T0276255

RANI
DURGAWATI

RANI DURGAWATI

The
FORGOTTEN LIFE
of a
WARRIOR
QUEEN

NANDINI SENGUPTA

PENGUIN
VIKING

An imprint of Penguin Random House

VIKING

USA | Canada | UK | Ireland | Australia
New Zealand | India | South Africa | China

Viking is part of the Penguin Random House group of companies
whose addresses can be found at global.penguinrandomhouse.com

Published by Penguin Random House India Pvt. Ltd
4th Floor, Capital Tower 1, MG Road,
Gurugram 122 002, Haryana, India

First published in Viking by Penguin Random House India 2022

ISBN 9780670094363

Typeset in Adobe Garamond Pro by Manipal Technologies Limited, Manipal
Printed at Thomson Press India Ltd, New Delhi

www.penguin.co.in

Dedicated with thanks to
Dr Suresh Mishra
Teacher, guide and fount of knowledge—without whose
unstinted help, this book would never have been possible.

And to my little daughter Aura,
Because every word I write, I write for you.

Contents

1

Remembering the Rani

'*Rani maharani jo aaye, Mata Durga jo aaye/Ran Ma jujho dhare tarwar Mata Durga kahaye*'

(Here comes the queen, here comes the goddess, always battle ready with sword in her hand she is called Mata Durga)

—Gond folk song (*Gond Kingdom of Garha*, 226)

The story of *Veerangana* Durgawati is a story of memories—of why she was remembered and why she was forgotten. Mainstream Indian history remembers her as a footnote—a tribal queen from central India who lost her kingdom to Mughal Emperor Akbar. But for her people, her memory is the gilded dream of an age of pride and plenty. It's been nearly 460 years since this brave queen made her final sacrifice, but her people have not forgotten her even for a day. Gond Rani Durgawati of Garha Mandla was and continues to be a symbol of hope. For the tribal Gonds who were her people, there has never been nor ever will be a more model monarch. This constant harking back to a golden age ruled by a goddess queen is understandable when seen in the context of the deprivation that the region suffered in the intervening centuries. Whenever the traditional way of life—from food to faith—came under attack, local memory, Gond and otherwise, remembered the rani.

And yet, curiously, Durgawati herself was not Gond. A Rajput princess of impeccable lineage, she married into the tribal Raj Gond dynasty. This was no political arrangement, however—the story of their whirlwind love lives on to this day in legend and song. The romance is unusual because royal inter-caste unions were not dime-a-dozen in medieval India. Indeed, Raj Gond history mentions only one other example, when dynasty founder soldier of fortune Yadurai or Yadavrai married Gond princess Ratnavali. Nor was this the only instance in which Rani Durgawati displayed era-defying spine and spunk. In fact, here was a medieval woman who seemed almost modern in the choices she made throughout her life. When her husband died leaving behind an infant heir, she took up the reins of her kingdom, fobbed off a grudging brother-in-law and handled her duties with competence. She chose her officials wisely, picking civil and military appointees not merely from the power pool that backed her in court, but also outsiders, including those whom she defeated in battle. She appointed and promoted a number of Muslim generals and officials displaying a degree of practical tolerance that mimicked what her Mughal adversary came to espouse and become famous for. Many of these men remained faithful to her till the very end, and a number of them lost their lives in the final battle. She used diplomatic distance when warranted and a bare-knuckled show of strength when the need arose. Indeed, till the Mughal general Asaf Khan burst on the scene armed with the imperial mandate to chop up the golden gourd that was Garha, she maintained cordial if distant relations with Akbar, exchanging scholars and gifts with the Mughal court. Yet when her neighbours tried to gobble up some of her land, she gave them a nose-bleed reply. Ultimately though, she's remembered for her righteous resistance to relentless bullying, for choosing sacrifice instead of survival in her final face-off. She fought till the bitter end knowing that the odds were stacked against her simply because it was 'better to die with glory than to live with ignominy'. Lion-hearted yet level-headed, spirited and shrewd, as courageous as she was compassionate, Gond Rani Veerangana Durgawati would have been an extraordinary woman in any age. That she lived in medieval India makes her story even more remarkable.

For someone so well endowed with both character and charisma, it's no surprise that the queen has attracted a fair number of admirers down the centuries, men who came to know her through her story and felt inspired by her spirit. Many of them were alien to the land she called her own, some were politically and militarily opposed to her, but not one of them grudged the queen her share of applause. Take British civilian William Henry 'Thuggee' Sleeman, who was among the most eloquent of the queen's eulogists. As a young administrator mapping central India through 1819–20, Sleeman stumbled across the stark and rugged boulder-strewn landscape that marked the precise spot of Durgawati's final moments on earth. It moved him so much that years later he described his feelings in the most poetic language possible.

He wrote in his *Rambles and Recollections of an Indian Official* sometime in 1835–36,

> The travellers who pass this solitary spot respectfully place upon the tomb the prettiest specimen they can find of the crystals which abound in the neighbourhood; and with so much of kindly feeling had the history of Dhurgoutee inspired me that I could not resist the temptation of adding one to the number, when I visited her tomb some 16 years ago . . .[1]

The legend of Dhurgoutee or Durgawati had cast a spell on Sleeman, and for the next decade-and-a-half he did not forget the brave queen and the haunting folk tales that remembered and revered her. 'Two rocks lie by her side which are supposed by the people to be her drums converted into stone,' wrote Sleeman, 'and strange stories are told of their being still occasionally heard to sound in the stillness of the night by the people of the nearest villages.'[2] Dhurgoutee, he added, 'reigned over a country where her name is not more revered than that of any other sovereign it has ever had.'[3]

Touching tribute indeed! Sleeman records some of medieval India's most colourful figures in his jottings but this Indian Boudica touched him like no other.

But who was Dhurgoutee or Durgawati, and why was Sleeman so moved by her story? Two hundred years after Sleeman chanced upon her samadhi in that desolate spot in the heart of India, Queen Durgawati remains an enigma. Although in folk song and local memory she remains a veerangana, the region's most enduring image of valour, she is little known outside central India, her gallantry and grit forgotten by the rest of us. But step into Jabalpur—and the surrounding districts of Narsinghpur, Hoshangabad, Mandla, Dindori, Damoh—and suddenly Durgawati comes alive through the mists of time. She is everywhere. Temples and tanks, roads and ruins bear her name with pride. Take Narai Nala, the spot whose haunting beauty so moved Sleeman. Just over a 100 years ago, local clergyman Eyre Chatterton photographed and described the queen's tomb in his book *The Story of Gondwana*. 'Her simple tomb, called appropriately by the villagers the Chabutra, about ten miles from Jubbulpore, is still held in reverence by all who live in its neighbourhood and by strangers who pass it by,' he wrote.[4] Chatterton's photograph shows no sign of a chabutra though—just a crumbling brick-laid platform with a single dried-up tree shooting out from it, its dead branches sharply outlined against the sky with thick forests lining the horizon.

Today, the spot looks very different indeed. Skirted by a bustling highway that pours a steady stream of selfie-happy visitors into a brick-and-grille low-walled enclosure, the Narai Nala samadhi *sthal* is a simple memorial that marks the spot where Rani Durgawati sacrificed her life for the sake of honour nearly 500 years ago on a rain-swept June day in 1564. Today, 24 June has become ingrained in the local consciousness as *balidaan diwas* or sacrifice day, a day when the local populace, both tribal Gond as well as otherwise, celebrate their most famous daughter with poetry and pomp, stories and song, dance and devotion. Even a pandemic didn't dent this enthusiasm—despite restrictions, the queen's anniversary was celebrated with tributes and solemn

ceremony in June 2020, 2021 and 2022. Interestingly, apart
from the official presence, many of those offering their respect
to the queen, whether at her samadhi or her likeness in the
university grounds, are women. They pray to her with flowers
and incense as the Gond bards sing songs remembering her
final sacrifice. Fierce and formidable, Durgawati is no coy
symbol of femininity. Whether clad in chain mail or a sari,
she is always battle ready, her naked sword a reminder of her
reputation as a warrior.

The memorial and its annual anointment apart, Rani
Durgawati's memory lingers in every nook and cranny of
this region. Back in 1916, Chatterton wrote about 'one
fine stretch of water between Jubbulpore and Garha' that
'still bears her name, the Rani Tal'.[5] Today, the fifty-two
water bodies she is credited with by local lore have mostly
disappeared, but there are other markers to her memory.
The city's cricket stadium is called Veerangana Durgawati
Stadium. Jabalpur's well-known university is named Rani
Durgawati Vishwavidyalaya. The city's favourite park,
Bhawartal Garden, boasts a statue of the rani astride her
black elephant Sarman, armed with a spear and wearing
full chain mail armour. The installation dominates the
manicured gardens all around, a reminder that nearly five
centuries on, the queen is still battle ready to protect her
people. One of the city's oldest hospitals, once bearing the
name of Lady Elgin, is now called Rani Durgawati Hospital.
Not too far away from Jabalpur, one of MP's smaller reserve
forests is called Veerangana Durgawati Wildlife Sanctuary,
and there is now a proposal to rename Jabalpur's revamped
Dumna airport after the Veerangana. Walk into the city

museum, and you will find exhibits dedicated to the queen's memory. Her fort, Rani Durgawati ka Kila or Madan Mahal, lies just a short drive out of the city. The Sharada Mata temple near the fort also remembers the queen through an annual pilgrimage. Local historians say the deity here was consecrated by Durgawati and became popular for wish fulfilment ever since the queen dedicated a red pennant to the goddess after defeating her neighbour Baz Bahadur, the sultan of Malwa. Since then, on every Monday in the month of Sawan (July–August), hundreds of devotees walk barefoot to this temple to offer the red pennants associated with both the queen and the goddess.

This isn't the only example of how the queen and the goddess from whom she takes her name have become intrinsically connected in local imagination. Many of the Gond songs that venerate Durgawati make little distinction between the queen and her celestial namesake. In the rousing extract given below, Rani Durgawati is described as an incarnation of 'Ran Chandi' or Goddess Durga.[6]

'*Tari nana, mor nana, rey nana/Rani Durgawati jo aaye. Mata Durga jo aaye./ Ran Ma jujhe dharey talwaar. Rani Durga kahaye. Tek/ Raja Dalpat key rani ho, Ran Chandi kahaye./ Dagar Dagar Ma dolon ho, Garh Mandla bachaye.*'

(Here comes the queen Durgawati. Here comes Mother Durga/She is battle ready with a sword in hand and she is called Rani Durga/She is Raja Dalpat's queen and she's like Ran Chandi, an incarnation of Goddess Durga/She is everywhere and she protects Garha Mandla.)[7]

Another song ends with people seeking blessings from the queen who was also the goddess.

'*Mata Durga Ran Chandi ke laybo charan pakhar/Hath jor binti karey ho, jay jay hovay tumhar*'

(Mother Durga is the incarnation of the Goddess Ran Chandi, and we should cling to her feet/pray to her with folded hands for victory.)[8]

Rani Durgawati also has other temples to her name, even though often the presiding deity is Shiva, not Shakti. One such temple stands in Barman, on the southern banks of the Narmada in Narsinghpur district and is called Rani Durgawati Temple. According to local lore, the temple was built by Rani Durgawati, even though historians say the current building is not particularly old and is probably the modern rebuilt version of an older structure that got washed away when the river flooded.[9]

Walk into the temple complex on the opposite bank of the river during the Makar Sankranti Mela in January, and you will be greeted by psychedelic lights and packed crowds. But on a normal weekday, it is possible to enter unjostled by crowds eager to click pictures of the elephant gate or offer their prayers as they crawl around and under the intricately carved Varaha statue in the courtyard. While the Prachin Narmada Mandir nearby is bigger and more popular with pilgrims, Durgawati's temple gets its fair share of devotees. Ask around, and nearly every one of them remember the queen and the story of her final sacrifice, even though the versions range from plain sketchy to wildly fantastic.

This reverence for local heroes is of course not unusual, particularly when the land itself is as redolent of *itihasa* and *sanskara* as the banks of the holy Narmada. But Durgawati's reputation isn't restricted to her own people—the brave queen earned respect from her enemies as well, historians who sided with those that tried to bludgeon her into submission and failed: Men who had no love for what they saw as her intransigence and, therefore, no need to sing her praises. Indeed her contemporary chroniclers have painted a picture of Durgawati that is unusually favourable. A queen who was not only brave and beautiful but also clear-headed and capable. In short, a model monarch.

A quick vox populi survey of sixteenth-century chroniclers shows just how definitively this praise was showered. Take Abul Fazl, whose detailed accounts in the *Akbarnama* form the most complete primary source of information on Rani Durgawati. The *Akbarnama* is a chronicle of the life and reign of Mughal Emperor Akbar—the man responsible for ordering the military offensive that cost Durgawati both her legacy and her life. The *Akbarnama* is a detailed and rich account, but as a hagiography commissioned by the emperor himself, it is also obviously biased in favour of the monarch, who was Abul Fazl's master and dear friend.

Yet this is the man who says about Durgawati,

At this time, when Asaf Khan became jagirdar of Sarkar Karra, and conquered the territory of Pannah, the sovereignty of that country (Gadha Katanga) had come to a woman named Durgawati, who was generally known as the Rani. She was distinguished for courage, counsel and munificence, and by virtue of these elect qualities she had brought the whole of that country under her sway.[10]

Abul Fazl's arch-rival Abdul Qadir Badauni is just as lavish while describing the queen. Rani Durgawati, he writes, was 'a lady of great loveliness and grace, and in the prime of beauty, who held the government of the place, came against him (Asaf Khan) with 20,000 horse and foot, and 700 powerful elephants, and fought an obstinately contested battle'.[11] Similar is the account in the *Tabaqat-I-Akbari* by Khwajah Nizamuddin Ahmad. Describing the kingdom of Garha Katinka (Gardha Katanga/ Garha Mandla), he says, 'The ruler of this country at that time was a woman named Rani Durgawati. She had a complete share of beauty and grace.'[12]

Remember, these men were some of the senior-most members of Emperor Akbar's court. Abul Fazl was the grand vizier, Abdul Qadir Badauni was the grand mufti and Khwaja Nizam-ud-Din Ahmad Bakshi was the son of Muhammad Muqim-i-Harawi. He was Akbar's Mir Bakhshi. Chatterton puts things in perspective when he outlines some of the prejudices of these venerable gents. 'Certainly by far the fullest and most interesting reference to old Gondwana is to be found in the writings of Abul Fazl, the Moslem chronicler of Akbar's days, although as a highly-cultured Moslem he clearly felt contempt for the ignorant aborigines of Gondwana,' he writes. Indeed, Abul Fazl dismisses Rani Durgawati's people with barely disguised contempt. 'In the vast territories of Hindustan there is a country called Gondwana,' writes Abul Fazl. 'It is the land inhabited by the tribe of Gonds, a numerous race of people, who dwell in the wilds, spend their time in eating and drinking and in the procreation of children . . . they are a very low race.'[13] Badauni is even more vicious, calling her subjects dogs of the country' who 'were very devoted to her'.

Remember also that we're talking about medieval India. A woman monarch confident enough not only to run her own kingdom but also to won't-blink eyeball the young Mughal Emperor (Akbar was just a few years older than her teenage son Bir Narayan when Durgawati fell) was not going to win plaudits for her feminist fire. Abul Fazl, in fact, tempers his early praise with some pretty caustic comments about the rani's 'arrogance', and Badauni's tone turns downright nasty later on, but more about that in subsequent chapters.

Indeed, Durgawati is seldom spoken of except in terms of esteem. Deccani historian Muhammad Qasim or Ferishta was born just a few years before Durgawati died. His description of her gives an indication of just how much reverence she elicited from her contemporaries all over central and south India. 'When Asuf Khan was raised to the rank of a noble of 5000 horses, and procured the government of Kurra Manikpoor, he obtained permission of the king to subdue a country called Gurra, at that time governed by a Rany whose name was Doorgawutty, as celebrated for her beauty as for her good sense.'[14]

Like her contemporary Mughal and Deccani chroniclers, Durgawati earned praise from another unlikely quarter— British civil servants touring and mapping what was then called the Central Provinces. Take James Forsyth, who earned some renown as a hunter and explorer in the late nineteenth century thanks to his extensive tours of central India, including the then-inaccessible Amarkantak, the source of the Narmada and Mahanadi rivers. Forsyth was barely twenty-four when he embarked on this tour. In *The Highlands of Central India*, he mentions Rani Durgawati with respect if not reverence.

'In 1564,' he writes, 'the great Akbar sent his lieutenant to reduce the Gond chieftain of Mandla. The Gond troops, led by the heroic Durgawati, the Rajput widow of the last chief, made a noble resistance to the invader near Jubbulpur but the battle at last going against them, their leader stabbed herself rather than suffer the disgrace of defeat.'[15]

Indeed, 235 years after Rani Durgawati's final sacrifice, the peace and prosperity that the Raj Gond dynasty fostered in the kingdom was visible enough for these British civil servants to comment upon. Around sixty-five years before Forsyth's exploration of the region, another British traveller, J.T. Blunt, wrote about Jabalpur and the surrounding areas in the late eighteenth century. He wrote,

> The thriving condition of the province, indicated by the appearance of its capital, 'demands from me a tribute of praise to the ancient princes of the country . . . under the fostering hand of a race of Gond princes, a numerous people tilled a fertile country and still preserve, in the neatness of their houses, in the number and magnificence of their temples, their ponds and other public works, in the size of their towns and in the frequency of their plantations, the undoubted signs of enviable prosperity.[16]

Written in the late 1790s, Blunt's account does not capture the kingdom of Garha Mandla at the height of its glory. The last king of the Raj Gond dynasty, Narharishah, had, by then, died in imprisonment in 1789. The 344-year-old Raj Gond reign had long flickered out. Yet the prosperity of the country elicited from him a 'tribute of praise'. Even more unusually, this praise came despite the racial superiority and casual disdain which often coloured the view of the intrepid English officials who tramped through this region. These were British bureaucrats not normally prone to showering wonderstruck words in favour of the local populace, particularly when that populace was primarily tribal.

Let's take a quick detour to listen in to what the average British civil servant thought about the Gonds as a people. Forsyth himself is quite age-appropriately racist, calling the Gondwana locals, 'naked or clothed in leaves, living in trees and practising cannibalism', even though by the 1860s (after it became the Central Provinces) the British administration was already driving 'that great civiliser of nations—the iron road' through 'the heart of its valleys and Manchester had prophetically fixed an eye on its black soil plains as a future field for cotton'.[17] The primary focus, for many of these fine gentlemen, was profit, not praise.

As for the serenading Sleeman, remember too that he pops up as Seeleeman Bahadur both in the ouster of the last nawab of Awadh, Wajid Ali Shah (Amjad Khan, playing the nawab in Satyajit Ray's *Shatranj ki Khilari*, mentions him several times in the most dulcet tones and disparaging terms) as well as in the succession altercation that led to the final sacrifice of another veerangana—Rani Lakshmibai of Jhansi. Yet this is the same man who not only talks about Rani Durgawati in deep purple prose but also records in great detail some truly romantic if spooky lore associated with her. The rani's tomb, he writes, 'is still to be seen in a narrow defile between two hills and a pair of large round stones, which stand near, are, according to popular belief, her royal drums turned to stone, which in the dead of night are still heard, resounding through the woods and calling the spirits of warriors from their thousand graves around her'.[18]

The reason for all this praise-gazing is to establish a single point—in terms of reputation, Gond Rani Durgawati was certainly no pushover, right up until the late nineteenth and early twentieth century. Chatterton, for instance, likens Durgawati to none other than Sita. 'From time to time in the history of India women have appeared, around whose lives a halo of romance must forever linger,' he writes.

> Who that has read the story of the Ramayan can ever forget Sita . . . the faithful wife, who wore the white flower of a blameless life. And Sita has had many spiritual daughters in succeeding ages whose faithfulness, courage, purity and devotion have added fresh laurels to Indian womanhood . . . It is in this noble company of Indian heroines that Dalpat Shah's young widow Durgawati is worthy to be placed.[19]

This veneration down the centuries makes it all the more inexplicable why the queen slowly but surely vanished from mainstream Indian consciousness in the last sixty-odd years. Apart from a solitary postage stamp released in 1988, there is not much popular interest in her. In contrast, fellow Rajput monarch Rana Pratap, also known for bravely refusing to buckle to Akbar's relentless bullying, has been commemorated with two postage stamps—in 1967 and 1998 respectively—and his commander Jhala

Manna was given one as well in 2017. Meanwhile, the rani's adversary, Akbar, has had countless books written about him, both in academic and narrative formats, from the redoubtable Vincent Smith's *Akbar the Great Mogul* to picture books for children. A casual look on Amazon, by no means a definitive yardstick, shows up more than fifty titles, including serious academic work, narrative history, historical fiction and children's titles. There have been at least five bestselling books in the last four years alone. In contrast, Amazon throws up barely seven titles on Rani Durgawati, many of them picture books for children. There are no current narrative history titles exclusively focused on her, and even the definitive historical fiction work, *Maharani Durgawati* by Vrindavan Lal Verma, was written nearly sixty years ago.

So why did we forget Rani Durgawati? Because she was a woman ruler? Or because her sprawling kingdom was in a remote inaccessible tribal belt? Indian history's male gaze is not unknown. Despite a long list of brave, powerful, capable, cunning, smart and sassy queens gracing our past, popular general knowledge skips from one 'the Great' to another, all invariably male. The only queen who bucks this trend is Lakshmibai. Others have been happily and largely ignored. Durgawati was one of the two women who dared to cock a snook at the great Mughal Akbar (Chand Bibi was the other). Given our reverence for this noble monarch, is it any surprise that his adversaries lie hidden in the long shadow he casts on our history?

A survivor not afraid to stand up for her rights, a warrior smart enough to use terrain to counter much larger manpower and artillery strength, a devoted mother and able administrator, Durgawati ranks right up there as one of India's most underrated monarchs. It's time we revisit her story. She deserves nothing less.

2

Garha: The Golden Gourd

'*Pahucho jahan gaur aur kola/Taji basey andhiyar khatola/
Dakshin dahine rahahi tilanga/Uttar basey Gadha Katanga.*'

(When you reach Gaur and Kola, you come across
Andhiyar Khatola which is present day Sagar-Damoh
region. Tilanga or Berar lies to its south while Gadha
Katanga lies to its north)

—Malik Muhammad Jayasi in
Padmavat (1540)

Gond Rani Durgawati's story is the story of her land, Garha.
Fringed by the serene Satpura range, blessed by the holy
Narmada river, this unspoilt terrain, its brave but simple
people and the long line of kings that ruled here are at the
heart of the queen's final sacrifice.

So where was the kingdom of Garha and why did the
mighty Mughal emperor, advised by one of his senior-most
generals, think it worthwhile to send an army of 10,000
horsemen through hostile and inaccessible terrain in order

to conquer this piece of land? Garha may not be terribly well-known today, but there are plenty of references to it in medieval and early modern accounts. Take Malik Muhammad Jayasi, the sixteenth-century poet who is experiencing a resurrection of sorts thanks to his epic *Padmavat* receiving a recent blockbuster Bollywood retelling. What is less known is that Jayasi's poem also throws in a few lines about the land ruled by Rani Durgawati and the dynasty she married into. Jayasi describes the precise location of Garha in this manner: '*Pahucho jahan gaur aur kola/Taji basey andhiyar khatola/ Dakshin dahine rahahi tilanga/Uttar basey Gadha Katanga.*'

This Gadha or Garha is the land of the Gonds. It is one of the four kingdoms that made up Gondwana, its mountains, forests and plains stretching between the Narmada and the Godavari. The kingdom of Chanda lay in the southern part of this region; the centre comprised Deogarh and Kherla. Garha, the domain of Durgawati, spanned northern Gondwana.

Tucked away in the heart of India, Garha is a place of jaw-dropping natural beauty and great antiquity, preserving nearby footprints of some of India's most illustrious kings from long-ago dynasties, from the Mauryas to the Guptas to the Chandelas. Not surprisingly, the colonial chroniclers who wrote about this region seemed enchanted by it. Chatterton, for instance, cannot believe how well-kept a secret this emerald kingdom is. 'Were one asked to describe the special charm of Gondwana,' he writes, 'one would, I think, at once point to the beautiful Satpura hills and plateaux, which lie at its very heart. Strange to say few . . . know of the real beauty which lies hidden away in this still rather inaccessible part of India.'

Chatterton wasn't the only man to be entranced by the 'splendid view' that greeted him in these lush lands punctuated by steep scarps and craggy outcrops. Nearly eighty years earlier—sometime in 1838 in fact—James Forsyth had been left spellbound when he first chanced upon the majestic troika of Satpura peaks, piercing the blue horizon and awash with all the colours of a dying day. 'Through the vistas of the trees, three great isolated peaks began to appear, glowing red and fiery in the setting sun against the purple background of a cloud-bank,' he wrote in *The Highlands of Central India*.

> The centre one of the three . . . was the peak of Mahadeo, deep in the bowels of which lies the shrine of the god himself; to the left, like the bastion of some giant's hold, rose the square and abrupt form of Chauradeo; while to the right, and further off than the others, frowned the sheer scarp of Dhupgarh, the highest point of these central Indian highlands.

Today, that point from where Forsyth first glimpsed the peaks is called Priyadarshini Point, renamed from the earlier Forsyth Point following a visit by former Prime Minister Indira Gandhi.

Natural beauty apart, this was also largely uncharted territory for Forsyth and he—wrongly as it turns out—assumed that 'the Great Akber knew nothing of the Gonds but as a people who tame lions so as to make them do anything they please and about whom many wonderful stories are told'.[1] The region remained an enigma even as late as 1853, as is evident from the way Sir Erskine Perry referred to it while addressing the Bombay branch of the Royal Asiatic Society. 'At present the Gondwana highlands and jungles comprise such a large tract of unexplored country that they form quite an oasis in our maps,' he said. This remoteness helped when the region wholeheartedly participated in the 1857 uprising, India's first war of independence. Although, as we shall see later, both the land and its lords had to pay a terrible price for it.

The British presence in the region, which began after the Third Anglo-Maratha War in 1818, took roots after 1857 and by 1861, things began to change—for the worse. Gondwana became part of the Central Provinces under the chief commissionership of Sir Richard Temple of the Bengal Civil Service. In 1865, a forest department was set up to classify different types of forests and to restrict access to reserved areas. The British wanted to tap forest produce and increase farm yield from this still relatively wild heart of India. These sledgehammer attempts at 'civilizing the savage' were catastrophic to say the least and led to a number of tribal uprisings right up to the 1930s. All through these decades of disruption, the Gond remembered their favourite rani, thanking her for giving her people the aspiration for a better life. Local historians say these pre-Independence Gond songs always painted the *gora* as the villain—a sharp contrast with the ideal monarch of yore.

To be fair, though Durgawati's acclaim as the goddess queen predates the arrival of the gora in Gondwana. Indeed, her reputation as an able ruler is so entrenched among the Gond people that there are stories about how it made even the young Mughal emperor curious about both the queen and the country. Legend has it that Durgawati's diwan Adhar Kayastha, who was invited by Akbar to the Mughal court, used a simple metaphor to explain Garha's defences, both military and natural, to the emperor. Garha, he said, was a ripe bitter gourd—its terrain rough and craggy like the gourd's skin, the golden colour representing its riches and the bitter taste a reminder of what invaders could expect if they attacked. While this may be an apocryphal story, it shows clearly that the people of Garha were quite well aware of their terrain advantage.

Indeed, the terrain was a critical and strategic aspect of the final battle at Narai Nala between Rani Durgawati and Asaf Khan. Abul Fazl gives a remarkably detailed description of the geography of the kingdom of Garha. 'In the vast territories of Hindustan, there is a country called Gondwana,' he writes.

> It is the land inhabited by the tribe of Gonds . . . The length of the district is 300 miles. On the north lies Panna. On the south the Deccan. On the west it borders on Raisin, belonging to Malwa, and on the east Ratanpur. The country is called Garha Katanka, and contains 70,000 villages. Garha is the name of its chief city and Katanka is the name of a place near it. These two places have given their names to the whole country.[2]

Historian Suresh Mishra gives a more up-to-date description of which parts of modern-day central India once comprised the kingdom of Garha. This includes the Malwa plateau, the Vindhya plateau, the Narmada–Sone river valley, the Satpura range, the Maikal plateau, parts of the Bundelkhand plateau and parts of Chattisgarh. The Malwa plateau formed the north-west corner of Garha, comprising modern day Bhopal, Raisen, Bidisha and Sagar districts. The Vindhya plateau, particularly the districts of Damoh and Katni, formed the northeastern fringe of Garha. It is also the site for one of the kingdom's most imposing forts. The rambling ruins of Singorgarh Fort in Singrampur village of Damoh district (Madhya Pradesh) mark one of the capital cities of Garha Katanga. Among the first things that Durgawati's husband Dalpati/Dalpat Shah did after taking over the reins following his father's death was to refurbish the fort and move the capital from Garha to Singorgarh in an effort to better secure his base. The *Gadhesh Nrpa Sangrah Shlokah*, an eighteenth-century literary anthology in Sanskrit, mentions this move saying: '*Nrpa Dalapati Shahi simhadurgay stithiarth*' (King Dalpati Shah lives in the Simhadurga fort). Mishra connects this slokah with an inscription on the fort that mentions the word 'Gajsinghdurg' (main elephant door), which may have later been corrupted to Singhdurg and then Singorgarh.

A day trip to this delightful spot—just a forty-five-minute drive out from Jabalpur city—is enough to convince anyone that Dalpati clearly knew what he was doing. The fort's steep and narrow access through a boulder-strewn, jagged and sometimes precipitous route snaking through the Bhander range of the Vindhyas is proof of why it was considered impregnable in its day. The forest cover, which was doubtless much thicker over 450 years ago, must have also been an important deterrent. Even today, there aren't that many visitors who brave the climb to check out the fort. Instead, the nearby waterfall gets the lion's share of picnickers. Part of the reason for that is also that this once imposing structure has now acquired the reputation of being haunted. The crumbling fort has fortunately just received some much-needed attention. In March 2021, President Ram Nath Kovind laid the foundation stone for conservation works at Singorgarh Fort and also inaugurated the newly carved Jabalpur Circle of the Archaeological Survey of India. Given how precarious the condition of the Singorgarh ruins are, this is welcome intervention indeed.

While mountains bordered the northern and southern margins of the kingdom, the heart of Garha Katanga was the fertile valley washed by two rivers, the Narmada and the Sone. This area currently covers the districts of Jabalpur, Narsinghpur, Hoshangabad and Harda. This strip of land is edged by the Bhander range in the north and the Satpura range in the south, which explains why the capital of the kingdom moved from Garha on the banks of the Narmada near the northern margin of these plains during Sangram Shah's rule, to Singorgarh in the far north during Dalpati Shah's reign, to Chauragarh tucked away in the even more inaccessible Satpura range when Durgawati was in charge.

Built around the 1540s by Sangram Shah—Rani Durgawati's powerful father-in-law—Chauragarh Fort or Chogan Kila as the locals call it, is a ghost of its former self today. Its remains lie in a crumbling heap on a picturesque hilltop that is hard to locate and harder to access. Just a mere 19 km from the temple town of Gadarwara in MP's Narsingpur district, the approach road to Chauragarh goes from tarred to mud track to rocky mountain pass pretty quickly, and only the very intrepid visitor, willing to trek right to the top of the hill up narrow hair-pin bends, will be rewarded with an entry into the fort. Once there, though, you are bound to lose yourself in the breathtaking vista that the ramparts offer.

This picturesque spot could have been a tourist attraction thanks to its location, the cloud-drenched greenery all around and the history and mystery associated with the ruins. Sadly, apart from two forlorn Archaeological Survey of India boards announcing that Chauragarh is a 'protected monument', there is no sign of any conservation effort anywhere. The tragedy of Chauragarh is that its neglect dates back centuries. Ironically, the reason for its current decay has a lot to do with its reputation as the treasure house of the Raj Gonds.

Clamber onto what was once the main building of the fort, and you realize how little of the original structure is still left standing and in what sorry condition. Covered in decaying leaves and garbage, tumble-down and broken bits of masonry lie scattered all around. Roofless walls stand tied up by a wild profusion of roots and creepers, crumbling doorways open on to sheer drops, bits and pieces of the stairway fall towards dank depths and end abruptly at the edge of a precipice. It is a sad testament to the fractured fortunes of this once imposing structure and the mighty monarchs that ruled from here. While official apathy is partly to blame, what's more unfortunate is that this fort was deliberately destroyed. Twice over.

After Asaf Khan defeated and killed Durgawati's teenage son Bir Narayan, he systematically and ruthlessly plundered Chauragarh. Given the loot it yielded, it is unlikely anything of any value was left behind. Yet local imagination has dreamt up a fantastic story about how, despite the sack, the most precious item in the Raj Gond treasury remained safely hidden. Right next to the fort is a water tank, now almost entirely covered in water hyacinth. Local lore says this is where the lords of Garha hid their philosopher's stone, the secret of the kingdom's incredible riches.

Coming back to the fort itself, in the mid-seventeenth century, Bundela Raja Jujhar Singh occupied Chauragarh after driving out the then Gond overlord Hirday Shah. Gondwana was, by then, a Mughal vassal state, and Shah Jahan was understandably angered by this perfidy, more so because Jujhar refused to pay up the hefty compensation demanded of him. So the emperor sent an army led by his son Aurangzeb to face off with Jujhar Singh. When faced with defeat, Jujhar blew up the guns in the fort, laid waste to large parts of it and fled towards the Deccan. He was killed en route but that's another story.

Nearly two hundred years later, the British, having secured Chauragarh from the Marathas, did pretty much the same thing using cannon fire to raze the structure to the ground. Given how remote and inaccessible this place is, it is likely that the British realized it would be difficult to properly secure Chauragarh. Hence that random act of vandalism to prevent it from turning into a Maratha hideout. Though this did not stop them from looking for the mythical philosopher's stone. Local legend says they used elephants to tramp through the tank but could not find what they were looking for. Although two links in the chain that secured the elephants did, or so the story goes, turn into solid gold!

This wild and rugged region, which also includes present-day Betul, Chhindwara and Seoni, once marked the southwestern edge of Garha Katanga. The southern side comprised the modern-day districts of Balaghat, Mandla and Dindori. This area juts into the Maikal plateau, which now boasts two national parks—Kanha and Satpura. The capital of Garha moved to this region after the fall of Chauragarh, first to Ramnagar and then to Mandla. Ramnagar was chosen in the mid-seventeenth century, after the Bundelas ousted the Raj Gonds permanently from Chauragarh (Jujhar Singh's shenanigans were just the thin end of the wedge) and around half a century on the capital moved to Mandla. The Bundelas continued to be a major thorn in the flesh of the Raj Gonds, but through all the ups and downs, Garha remained at the heart of much power and passion play. Indeed, nearly 165 years after Durgawati, a powerful Maratha general, who was camping in Garha at that time, went to the aid of a besieged Bundela Raja. The name of the general was Bajirao, and the man he rode off to help was Chattrasaal, father of Mastani. Both Bajirao and Mastani, of course, have also gained popularity in recent years as the protagonists of another Bollywood screen epic.

The Bundelas were natural allies and also enemies of the Raj Gonds because a tiny edge of Garha extended to the northern districts on the Maikal plateau which come under Bundelkhand. Garha also included the modern-day districts of Nagpur and Bhandara, which formed the southern-most stretch of the kingdom. This region became the base for the Maratha Bhonsles by the fag end of the seventeenth century, by which time the Raj Gonds were a ghost of their former selves.

This, then, was the precise location of the territory commanded by the Raj Gond monarchs when Durgawati came to power between 1548 and 1550. Thickly forested, this region was not easy to penetrate and had till then remained untouched by outside invasion. Abul Fazl mentions this while documenting Rani Durgawati's dominions: 'The seat of government is the fort of Chauragarh. The fighting men of this country are chiefly infantry, horsemen being few. From the earliest establishment of the Mohammedan power in India no monarch has been able to reduce the fortresses of this country, or annex its territory.'[3]

So why was this remote forest kingdom important enough for Akbar's senior general Asaf Khan to covet? The answer is simple, really—Garha was an enormously rich kingdom. The fact that it had remained more or less unmolested by invaders for nearly a century when Durgawati came to power means that it was a settled dominion where wealth had been allowed to accumulate. Just how wealthy this kingdom was will become clear from one stray example.

The compact structure of Madan Mahal in Jabalpur is a must-visit tourist spot today. Apart from its stark architectural charm, this precariously placed palace, perched on a hilltop next to two giant boulders, is also a local favourite for treasure hunts. According to legend, Raj Gond monarchs, either Sangram Shah or Durgawati, buried a significant part of their fabulous wealth in one of the subterranean tunnels running under Madan Mahal. This fabulous claim, however, is partly rooted in history. Over a hundred years ago, in 1908 to be precise, this general area did yield a huge haul of gold and silver coins. The *District Gazetteer of Jubbulpore* describes the treasure in some detail 'A treasure trove was found in 1908, between Garha and Madan Mahal consisting of 146 gold and 36 silver coins,' reports the Gazetteer. 'Almost all of them are Muhammadan, bearing the names of the Sultans of Delhi, Gujarat and Kashmir and the Bahmanis of Kulbarga, the Khiljis of Malwa and the Sharqis of Jaunpur, ranging in date from 1311 to 1553. Three of the gold coins are suspected to be Nepalese.'[4]

That haul isn't surprising given the multiple contemporary references to the Garha wealth. Abul Fazl mentions that the Gond feudatories paid their tributes in gold mohurs, copper coins or elephants and that a large tract of Garha was densely forested, where herds of elephants roamed freely. Elephants, he says, were common in 'the forests stretching from Narwar to Berar and in Handia, Uchchod, Chanderi, Satwas, Bijagarh, Raisen, Hoshangabad, Garha and Hariagarh in the Malwa suba'. The Garha region, he adds, also had thick forest cover teeming with a large elephant population. Today, this region boasts several reserved forests, including Bori, Fen, Nauradehi, Pachmarhi, Ratapani, Singhori and, of course, the one named after the Gond Rani—Durgawati. Given how critical elephants were in medieval warfare, this would have been an important source of Garha's wealth. Indeed, Asaf Khan's Chauragarh loot included, apart from heaps of gold, silver and gems, 1,000 elephants. One of the reasons that led to his later rift with Akbar was the fact that he sent just 200 of these animals to the Mughal court, keeping the rest for himself. Later Gond rulers like Prem Narayan also won favour at the Mughal court by paying elephantine tributes, both literal and otherwise. Mughal emperor Jahangir documents this in his memoirs, saying that in the twelfth year of his reign (1617), 'the Raja of Garha Prem Narayan had the good fortune to wait on me and made an offering of seven elephants male and female', and in the same year he was 'promoted to a mansab of 1000 personal and 500 horse'.[5]

And yet the irony of Garha is that its wealth brought nothing but misfortune, both to itself as well as to the invaders. Take Asaf Khan. The loot he amassed after his conquest of Garha was sizeable enough to verily turn his head. Abul Fazl describes the hoard with some understandable tut-tutting about what greed does to one's good sense. After the fort of Chauragarh was captured, writes Abul Fazl, 'there fell into the hands of Asaf Khan and his men an incalculable amount of gold and silver. There were coined and uncoined gold, decorated utensils, jewels, pearl figures, pictures, jeweled and decorated idols, figures of animals made wholly of gold' and 'one hundred jars full of Allauddin's asharafis'.*

Indeed so huge was the loot that Fazl calls it 'senses robbing intoxication', which made Asaf Khan abandon 'the path of propriety' so that he 'sent none of those rarities or splendid jewels, which were worthy of the appreciative acceptance of the Shah-in-shah, to court'. Abul Fazl turns positively apoplectic with indignation at this perfidy, writing that Khan 'did not comprehend that fortune had made those pearls and jewels a sprinkling for the head of dominion and a tiara for the auspicious, and regarding himself as the central object, he strewed the dust of ruin on the head of his own honour'. This flowery reprimand is proof that Chauragarh

---

* Ashrafis are medieval gold coins.

yielded so much gold and silver that even a seasoned Mughal official such as Asaf Khan was willing to risk Akbar's wrath for the treasure.[6]

The tragedy of Garha was that its riches could well have been the reason for its fall. Abul Fazl is frank enough when he explains that Asaf Khan and his men were propelled as much by the imperial diktat as by the lure of loot during the attack on Chauragarh. 'This fortress was replete with buried treasures and rare jewels for the collection of which former rajahs had exerted themselves for many ages,' he writes. 'They thought these would be a means of safety but in the end they were a cause of destruction. The soldiers girded upon the loins of courage to capture this golden fort, and from the love of these treasures they washed their hands of life and eagerly followed Asaf Khan.'[7]

The plundering, in fact, continued even after the conquest was over and Garha became a vassal state of the Mughal empire. Veteran historian Dr Subhash Chandra Sharma, head of the Department of History at the Rani Durgavati Vishwavidyalaya, Jabalpur, explains what happened. 'After Durgawati, Gondwana's prosperity started fading away. First Asaf Khan's victorious army looted as much as they could, and then successive Mughal officials appointed by Akbar extorted it, squeezing the common folk.' As a result, the once supremely wealthy Garha became a revenue laggard under Mughal rule. Interestingly, information about this comes from the *Ain-i-Akbari* itself. For a relatively large kingdom comprising fifty-seven mahals (Ujjain in comparison had ten mahals, Sarangpur twenty-four, Mandu sixteen, Nadurbar seven and Handia twenty-three), Garha's income was just

10,077,080 dams. In comparison, Ujjain had an income of 43,827,960 dams, Sarangpur 32,994,880 dams, Mandu 13,788,994 dams, Handia 11,610,969 dams and Nadurbar 50,162,250 dams.[8] (The dam was the copper coin in use in medieval India along with the silver coin called rupee/rupaiya and gold coin called muhur.)

The frequent transfer and short tenure of Mughal jagirdars and their tendency to exploit the peasantry for personal and state benefit is well documented. The fact that a succession of Mughal jagirdars were appointed to Garha in the three decades after Asaf Khan—including the likes of Mahdi Quasim Khan, Shah Quli Khan, Kakar Ali Khan, Sadiq Khan, Baqui Khan, Mirza Aziz Koka, Shaham Khan among others—shows that this trend would have bled Garha dry too. Worse, Durgawati's successors began to lose territory, so the kingdom shrank. It began with Chandra Shah, Durgawati's brother-in-law, who offered the Mughals ten districts as tribute when he staked his claim to the throne. These districts later became the principality of Bhopal. 'All of this dealt a body blow to the social, political and economic health of Gondwana,' says Sharma.

By the first decades of the twentieth century, this nearly 400-year-old depredation of Gondwana started showing up in Gond songs as well. In the 1935 anthology *Songs of The Forest: Folk Poetry of the Gonds* by Shamrao Hivale and Verrier Elwin, there are heart-rending poems that talk of famine and starvation. '*This year's famine has driven us mad/What are we to do brothers, what are we to do? We get no profit on our sowing/ We cannot even reap what we have sown/Come let us go with our baskets bare of grain.*'[9] This heart-stopping deprivation is in sharp contrast to Garha's legendary prosperity under Raj Gond rulers like Durgawati and her father-in-law Sangram Shah. This wealth came not only from elephants, but other forest produce as well, which is repeatedly referenced in local bard song. Gond folklore often talks about local kings paying a tribute of wild nuts and berry liquor to the Muslim emperor in Delhi. For example, local legend says King Premnarayan/Prem Shah of Garha was once summoned to the imperial court in Delhi. He went there carrying mahua liquor and chironji seeds, both common forest produce in the region to this day. Another folk tale talks of Gond king Bodhanshah, brother of Prem Shah's son Hirday Shah mentioned earlier. This king sent five pots of rice, five pots of tendu and water chestnuts, five pots of honey and five pots of chironji nuts as tribute to Mughal emperor Aurangzeb.[10] Forest produce apart, Garha also exported foodgrain to neighbours in the west and south and the fertile Narmada–Sone valley was the local grain basket. Abul Fazl mentions this while speaking of Garha: 'By its cultivation the Dakshin and Gujarat obtain relief.'[11]

Local historians say Garha's produce, forest and farm grown, must have been exported extensively, which explains the wide variety of coins that popped up in the Madan Mahal treasure mentioned earlier. Given how remote Garha was, coins from Gujarat, Kashmir, Kulbarga in the Deccan, Jaunpur, Malwa and even Nepal, apart from Sultanate dinars from Delhi, being found here can only mean one thing— Garha was a rich trading centre back in the Middle Ages. This wealth is also part of the reason why Rani Durgawati had to fend off attacks from Baz Bahadur of Malwa and the Miyana Afghans before Asaf Khan's final assault. A rich kingdom ruled by a woman would have been seen as easy prey by the predatory neighbours who surrounded Garha, making it a magnet for invasions and border skirmishes. In the end, Garha's prosperity, and the stable administration that ensured it, also led to its downfall. Yet it is to the rani's credit that her tightly knit kingdom continued for more than 200 years after her death, surviving the Mughal invasion as well as the tumult of the eighteenth and nineteenth centuries. Not surprisingly, 450 years on, her presence is still visible all over central India. Take the song *Mor Durgawati O Garh Mandla Ki Rani* by DJ Sarman released in 2020. A panegyric of the Veerangana, it talks about not only her courage and sacrifice but also the prosperity her rule brought about. '*Puri raj ma soney ki sikka*', or a kingdom covered by gold coins, is too fantastic a claim to be true, but for the locals of Gondwana, that's the aspiration the rani still stands for. For the golden gourd kingdom of Garha, Rani Durgawati is both model monarch and patron saint. Her story is now the story of her land. Her memory infuses every rock face and ruin, every temple and tank. Sleeman describes best what this brave daughter meant and still means to her people: 'Of all the sovereigns of this dynasty she lives most in the page of history and in the grateful recollection of the people.'[12]

3

Lord of Bhavan Garh—Amhandas/ Sangram Shah

'Kahan gaye Raja Amhan, ban ki rovay chiroya?

(Where did he go Raja Amhan, the birds in the forest cry)

—Gond folk song

The year was 1917. Rai Bahadur Hiralal, Jabalpur's historian extraordinaire, was researching his seminal book *Jabalpur Jyoti*, when he came across a sati stone in a deserted and remote village called Tharraka, 15 miles or 24 km from Damoh district of Madhya Pradesh. The stone had an inscription dated Samvat 1570 (1513 CE), which referred to a monarch called 'Maharaja Shri Amandas Deo'.[1] This was not the first time that Amandas or Amhandas called out his name from the depths of time, however. More than half a century before Rai Bahadur Hiralal, American orientalist Fitz Edward Hall had presented a translation of a medieval inscription found in Ramnagar (in Mandla district) to the *Journal of the American Oriental Society*. Dated 17 October 1860 and groaning under the somewhat bombastic title *On the Kings of Maṇḍala, As Commemorated in a Sanskrit Inscription Now First Printed in the Original Tongue*, this translation talked about a king called Sangram Shah or Sangramasahi in the most glowing terms. Son of Arjunasinha (Arjundas), this Sangramasahi, said the inscription, was

> an exterminating fire to his foes, as if they had been masses of cotton-wool: on the radiance of whose grandeur being spread abroad, the midday sun became like a mere spark. By which king, when he had reduced the orb of the earth, two and fifty fastnesses were constructed; indestructible from their excellent fortifications . . . and because of their water.

Powerful words indeed, particularly since the inscription has been dated around 1667 (during the reign of later Gond monarch Hirday Shah), more than 125 years after the death of the king who was born Amhandas and later called himself Sangram Shah. Father of Dalpati Shah and father-in-law to Gond Rani Durgawati, Sangram Shah was lord of fifty-two *garhas* and by all means a powerful sovereign, clearly feted for his military might during his lifetime and immediately afterwards. Even if we make allowances for the Ramnagar panegyric's flowery hyperbole, the expansion of the kingdom of Garha during the reign of Sangram Shah is proof enough that his strong arm was the reason why Durgawati inherited a kingdom as vast and stable as she did. Before him, Garha was just one of the many Gond kingdoms in Gondwana. After him, it became *the* Gond kingdom.

Sleeman[2] gives us an idea of just how impressive his military expansions were. 'At the close of the reign of Sangram Shah the dominion of the Garha Mandala rajas extended over fifty-two districts but it is believed that he received from his father only three or four of these districts,' he writes quite categorically. We will, of course, discuss the true dimensions of these fifty-two garhas shortly, but clearly Sangram Shah was a formidable political and military power in his day and was probably the reason why his son's short-lived seven-year rule remained uneventful and largely aggression-free. His daughter-in-law Durgawati also reaped the benefits of Sangram Shah's renown for realpolitik, at least in her initial years as regent, which were singularly peaceful despite the hostility of her neighbours.

Apart from the Ramnagar inscription, another near-contemporary work, the *Gadhesh Nripa Varnam* composed by eighteenth-century poet Rupnath Jha, reaffirms the view that Sangram Shah's kingdom was both rich and powerful. Indeed, the *Gadhesh* attributes his success in negotiating the topsy-turvy power play of the times to a divine boon—the ultimate compliment for a medieval king. The king's father Arjunsimha, says the *Gadhesh*, 'ruled for 32 years; who had a son born Sangramasahi who acquired the royal signs inward and who having obtained a boon from Bhairava enjoyed the royal pleasures for 50 years'. And in a word-by-word echo of the Ramnagar inscription, Rupnath Jha describes the extent of the kingdom thus: 'By him were built lands conquered from kings, 52 prominent forts furnished with mountain-high ramparts as also by ditches full of water.'[3]

Beyond the fifty-two garhas conquered by Sangram Shah, the most interesting part of this shloka is the boon it mentions. There is a popular and persistent story about Sangram Shah that connects him with his favourite temple and its presiding deity. Every historian, from Sleeman to Suresh Mishra, has recorded and referenced this story, so there may have been a historical core to it, though covered in romantic imagery. The story goes that an evil tantric lived in the famous Bajnamath Temple in Jabalpur, which was built by Sangram Shah himself and continues to be connected to his name in local memory. This tantric had attempted to offer the king as a human sacrifice to the deity. Sleeman describes what was supposed to have happened thereafter with his usual flourish.[4] Sangram Shah, he wrote,

> formed near the city of Gurha the great reservoirs called, after himself the Sangram Saugor and built on the bank of it the temple called the Bajnamath, dedicated to Bhyro, the god of truth. Tradition says that a religious mendicant took up his residence in this temple soon after it had been dedicated with the intention to assassinate the prince in fulfilment of a vow he had made.

Sleeman is clear that the tantric took advantage of both the prince's piety as well as his ambition and persuaded Sangram Shah 'that he could by certain rites and ceremonies so propitiate the deity . . . as to secure his aid in extending his conquests over all the neighbouring states. These rites and ceremonies were to be performed at night when no living soul but himself and the prince might be present'. After several discussions on the matter, the tantric finally managed to convince the prince and 'appointed the night and the hour' when the ceremonies were to take place.

What happened thereafter, even if this be but folklore, shows just how finely honed Sangram Shah's survival instincts were.

> Just as Sangram Shah was at midnight preparing to descend from his palace to the temple, one of his domestics entered his apartment and told him that he had watched this Sanyasi priest very closely for some time, and from the preparations he was now making he was satisfied that he intended to assassinate him.

Forewarned, Sangram Shah went to the temple 'alone but armed with a sword under his cloak'. The tantric asked the prince to walk around a fire 'over which was placed a boiling cauldron of oil', and then fall 'prostrate before the God'. But a keen-eyed Sangram Shah caught a glimpse of 'a naked sword' tucked away under the priest's robes, which confirmed his suspicions.

Sangram Shah now decided to turn the tables on the tantric and told him with creditable presence of mind, 'In rites like these it is no doubt highly important that every ceremony should be performed correctly, and I pray you to go through them first.' The priest did so, and when he lay down before the deity, Sangram Shah neatly chopped his head off. 'The blood spouted from the headless trunk upon the image of the God of truth.' The murti came to life and asked the prince to crave a boon. Sangram Shah, prostrating himself, said, 'Give me I pray thee victory over all my enemies as thou hast given it me over this miscreant.' Lord Bhyro asked him to adopt a brown flag and follow a jet black horse from his stable and thus do a medieval version of the Ashwamedha Yagna, which helped him conquer fifty-two formidable fortress districts.

What this legend suggests is that there was perhaps an attempt on the king's life and also that there may have been good reason for that attempt to be made. To understand why, we need to trace back the rather morally dubious route that Amhandas took to become king. Amhandas was the son of Gond king Arjundas/Arjun Singh, but he rebelled against his father and had to run away from Garha. The disgraced prince then sought refuge with Baghel Raja Vir Singh Dev of Rewa, a kingdom to the north-east of Garha. What led to this rift between father and son? In the Akbarnama,[5] Abul Fazl says that Amhandas was a 'trickster and evildoer. He always acted against the will of his father and prepared for himself eternal loss'. Even if we discount the bias and disapproval in Abul Fazl's tone, clearly there was bad blood between the two, which prompted the father to keep his son 'in confinement for some while and then let him out upon conditions' but once out, 'the wretch went back to his old courses and did improper acts'.

The rap on his knuckles did not work, and Amhandas finally ran away from Garha. When he sought refuge with Vir Singh, the Baghel king 'adopted him' says Abul Fazl. From all accounts, there was perfect camaraderie between the two, and when Vir Singh 'entered the service of Sultan Sikandar Lodi', he left Amhandas with his son 'Vir Bhanu, the father of Raja Ram Chand who was then young'.[6](Around fifty years later, this same Ram Chand would first defy the Mughals and then be defeated by Asaf Khan, paving the way for the imperial forces to land up at Durgawati's doorstep.) During this time, Amhandas 'outwardly followed a course of rectitude', says Abul Fazl. But then something happened. The prospect of a rebellious heir lurking among his neighbours would have made Arjundas understandably uneasy, so he decided to declare his second son Jogidas as the heir apparent. Jogidas, however, had 'respect to the claim of his elder brother and did not agree to this arrangement'.

At this point, Abul Fazl's story turns particularly blood-soaked. When he came to know what his father was planning Amhandas decided to intervene before Arjundas could formally gift the kingdom away to his younger son. The prospect of losing his inheritance, says Fazl, prompted him to make a 'rapid expedition'. He 'got into his mother's house and remained hidden there. With the concurrence of one of the Rajah's intimates, with whom he had old relations, he one night got his opportunity and killed the Rajah'.[7]

As can be imagined, this act of patricide did not go down well. 'The people rose and imprisoned him,' says Abul Fazl. They 'sent a messenger to the second son, but he would not accept the invitation, saying that he could not kill his elder brother, whom he regarded as a father, nor could he submit to him as he had prepared eternal loss for himself'. Jogidas thus 'elected retirement and went off into the desert'. The old raja's companions then wrote to Baghel Raja Vir Singh and invited him to take over the country. Vir Singh took leave of absence from Sikandar Lodi and 'marched with a force into the country', forcing Amhandas to run away into the mountains. At this point, the disgraced prince showed early signs of his prodigious survival instincts. Realizing that a faceoff with Vir Singh could cost him both his legacy and his life, he decided to surrender. He told the Baghel Raja that 'he had from ignorance and a disordered brain killed one father, and how could he now fight with a second?'.

This was smart thinking, because Vir Singh had already 'conquered the country and was returning after leaving his own men in charge', says Abul Fazl. Amhandas intercepted him and paid 'homage to him. After much lamentation, the Raja forgave him and made over the country to him. Amhandas wept continually and expressed his abhorrence of himself for his evil action'. This sudden self-loathing seems both over-the-top and too convenient to be anything but deft political footwork, and Abul Fazl sees it as such. 'Nor is it known whether this was hypocrisy or he became aware of his wickedness and so expressed his feeling of shame before God and men,' he says.[8]

Abul Fazl's dire disapproval notwithstanding, there is reason to believe this incident to be true because another contemporary work mentions it. The *Virabhanudayakavyam,* a poetic panegyric of the Baghela rulers written around 1540, says Virasimha or Vir Singh, 'set out against the ruler of Gadha who at once fled away before him. Thereupon, he resided at Gadha for some time and enjoyed baths in the Narmada river'.[9]

The very public soul searching helped Amhandas secure both his kingdom and Vir Singh's friendship, a remarkable feat given that he was, at this point, standing with his back to the wall. The next instance when Amhandas displayed similar diplomatic shrewdness was when he helped Sultan Bahadur Shah of Gujarat invade neighbouring Raisen. Raisen would, in the next several decades, become a key factor influencing the fortunes of Garha, as we shall see later. According to Abul Fazl, a grateful Bahadur Shah honoured Amhandas by conferring upon him the title of Sangram Shah.

There is some confusion about this though. Bahadur Shah's attack on the fort of Raisen happened on 10 May 1532. But Sangram Shah's coins bear this title from as far back as 1516. That was just two years after Amhandas did Ibrahim Lodhi, the ruling sultan in Delhi, a huge favour. According to the *Tarikh-i-Salatin-i-Afghana*, when Ibrahim Lodhi became sultan, his rebel brother Jalal escaped to Malwa. He first sought help from the Khalji ruler of Malwa, Mahmood Khalji, who wisely sidestepped the request. Jalal then fled to Garha Katanga, where the Gonds promptly captured him and Amhandas handed him over to Ibrahim Lodhi. Jalal was executed in 1518. So Amhandas could have adopted the title after earning himself some royal favours from Delhi very early on in his reign. What these incidents prove, though, is just how sharp Sangram Shah was and how well he navigated the treacherous undercurrents of the day.

After the initial ups and downs, Sangram Shah settled into a largely peaceful reign. He had two queens, Padmawati and Sumati, and two sons, Dalpati and Chandra. One of Dalpati's inscriptions refers to Padmawati Mai, so she was clearly his mother, and since he was the heir, she was probably the chief queen. But as is not unusual, Sangram Shah shows greater fondness for his other queen by making a dedication to her in his book *Ras Ratnamala*: '*Vame Hemavati saman*

Sumati, shri shahimatya yutah' (I have Sumati by my side who is like goddess Lakshmi herself). Either way, he probably had a happy family life because there are no references, even in folk accounts, of any bad blood between the two princes. That is just as well, given how tortuous the political situation of the region was at this time.

Sangram Shah's conflict-free reign has to be seen in the context of the Mughals and their connections with central India around this time. The Baghel rulers had an on-again off-again relationship with the Mughals going back to Babur, who mentions Vir Singh (or Bir Sing Deo) in the *Baburnama* as the monarch who went to the aid of Rana Sanga in their mutual confrontation at the battle of Khanwa.[10] Vir Bhanu, on the other hand, received felicitations from Humayun for the birth of his son Ram Chand (though this did not secure Raja Ram Chand's fortunes during the early years of Akbar's rule). The *Virabhanudayakavyam* talks about Humayun congratulating Vir Bhanu thus: 'The illustrious Humayun, who was the overlord of the Yavanas, the lord of Delhi and crest-ornament of kings, on hearing that a son was born to the son' of Vir Singh, 'became very pleased'. He regarded Vir Bhanu 'as his brother, and being delighted, he sent by his own ministers auspicious ornaments, horses, garments and scents'.[11] Sangram Shah maintained perfectly cordial relations with his Baghel friends but, unlike them, he remained largely neutral when it came to Humayun. Although he died shortly after Sher Shah Suri took over (either in 1542 or 1543), this neutrality ensured Garha remained mostly unmolested during Islam Shah Suri's rule.

When Sangram Shah came to the throne (around 1510, says Suresh Mishra, going by his coinage), Gond control was restricted to the country around Jabalpur and Mandla. To this, he added chunks of the fertile Narmada valley, including the districts of Damoh, Sagar, Seoni, Chhindwara and Narsimhapur as well as large portions of the territory which was later chopped off to create Bhopal state after the fall of Durgawati. Historians from Sleeman to Suresh Mishra have outlined the exact locations of the fifty-two garhas that Sangram Shah controlled. A quick laundry list of those districts at this point tells us just how far he expanded his rule.

1. Garha: Jabalpur suburb
2. Marugarh on the banks of the Balai river: 8 km from Kalpi on the Mandla–Jabalpur connector
3. Pachelgarh: the area around what is currently Sihora town of Jabalpur district
4. Singorgadh in Damoh district: this still houses the ruins of the impressive fort located around 45 km from the village of Sigrampur or Singrampur said to have been named after Sangram Shah. One version of the local legend says it was originally called Sangrampur, a name that referenced both the monarch's title as well as the origin of the place as a battleground.
5. Amoda: the area around Katangi in Jabalpur district
6. Kanauja: Jabalpur district
7. Baghmar: around the Kawardha district of Chhattisgarh
8. Tipagarh: in Balaghat district
9. Raigarh: the northeast region of Kawardha district, Chhattisgarh

10. Partabgarh: a section of Bilaspur district, Chhattisgarh
11. Amargarh: around 20 km south-west of Dindori in Madhya Pradesh
12. Deohar: near Shahpur in Dindori district of MP
13. Patangarh: area to the north-east of Jabalpur
14. Fatehpur: in Hoshangabad district, near Sohagpur tehsil
15. Nimuagadh: west Narsinghpur district
16. Bhanwargarh: in Narsinghpur district
17. Bargi: south Jabalpur
18. Ghansaur: in Seoni district of Madhya Pradesh
19. Chaurai: in east Chhindwara district
20. Dongartal: north-west of Nagpur
21. Karwargarh: west of the Wainganga river in Seoni district
22. Jhanjhangadh: in Jabalpur district, around 10 km from Bahuriband
23. Lafagadh: near Ratanpur, which is in Bilaspur district of Chhattisgarh
24. Santagarh
25. Diyagarh: in Jabalpur district on the banks of the Mahanadi
26. Bankagadh
27. Pawai Karhi: south Panna, at the edge of the Damoh district border
28. Shahnagar: boundary of Panna and Jabalpur district
29. Dhamauni: in Sagar district
30. Hata: north Damoh district
31. Madiadau: in Damoh district
32. Gadhakota: in Sagar district
33. Shahgadh: around 65 km from Sagar
34. Gadhpahra: near Sagar

35. Damoh
36. Rehli: in Sagar district
37. Itwa: north-east region of Sagar district
38. Kimlasa: north-west Sagar
39. Ganaur: south Bhopal
40. Bari: Raisen district
41. Choukigadh: Bhopal district
42. Rahatgadh: west Sagar
43. Makrai: south Harda
44. Karoobagh: Raisen district
45. Kurwai: Vidisha district
46. Raisen
47. Bhanwaraso: Vidisha district
48. Bhopal
49. Opadgadh: near Bhopal
50. Poonagadh: Narsinghpur district
51. Deori: south of Sagar
52. Gourjham: Sagar district

The list shows that the kingdom included the present-day districts of Jabalpur, Raisen, Harda, Hoshangabad, Narsinghpur, Katni, Damoh, Sagar, Seoni, Chhindwara, Mandla, Dindori and Balaghat. It also included the southern part of Panna district, the eastern part of Vidisha district and Bhopal, all in Madhya Pradesh, extending up to north-west Bilaspur, the Kawardha, Baghmar and Raigarh regions of Chhattisgarh and north-west Nagpur. Deogarh too was part of Sangram Shah's kingdom for at least a decade. Copper coins from the Deogarh mint, with Sangrama (Sa)hi Devag(arh) inscribed on them and a tiger with its tail raised on the obverse, show that from 1518 to 1529, Deogarh too was controlled by Garha Mandla.[12]

Sangram Shah's military and diplomatic quick-step becomes even more creditable when seen against the choppy fortunes of some of the regions he added to his kingdom. Take Raisen. Just three years after Bahadur Shah took over this territory—with the help of Sangram Shah—he was defeated by Humayun, and seven years later Sher Shah took over this region and appointed Shujaat Khan as its governor. Raisen became part of the Mughal empire when Akbar defeated Baz Bahadur, Shujaat Khan's son. According to historian Suresh Mishra, this political turmoil meant that a part of Raisen (around nine fort districts or garhas) actually paid tribute to and considered itself under the protection of the more stable and powerful Sangram Shah. Given how well-versed in realpolitik he was, it would have been unimaginable for Sangram Shah not to fish in Raisen's troubled waters next door.

Sangram Shah ruled for more than three decades at least—a long, peaceful reign that allowed him time to focus on both trade and agriculture. This helped Garha become one of the wealthiest kingdoms in central India. Gold, silver and copper coins bearing his name have been found, which is unusual, because in medieval India 'very few Hindu and Rajput kings minted their own coins', says Suresh Mishra.[13] But Sangram Shah minted gold coins three times during his reign, which begs the question, how did the ruler of a remote and inaccessible kingdom have enough gold to mint coins at a time when there are barely any references to more well-known Rajput kingdoms minting their own?

Clearly thanks to trade in forest produce and agricultural exports to markets such as Gujarat, Garha was a prosperous kingdom. The stability of Sangram Shah's rule further filled its coffers. Indeed, Abul Fazl says quite categorically that the reason Durgawati's father accepted Dalpati as his son-in-law was because of Garha's prodigious prosperity, 'though he (Dalpati) was not of a good family yet as he was wealthy and Rajah Salbahan was in bad circumstances, the latter was compelled to make this alliance', says the *Akbarnama*.[14] Sleeman explains things better when he says, 'under the easy eventless sway of these (Gond) princes, the rich country over which they ruled prospered, its flocks and herds increased and the treasury filled'.

That the kingdom was both peaceful and prosperous also becomes obvious from the number of Sanskrit scholars who were patronized by Sangram Shah. The king himself was a writer of some repute, and his *Ras Ratnamala* is a fine treatise on kingship and politics. He also started the practice of inviting learned men from elsewhere to settle down in his kingdom, which his daughter-in-law reverentially continued. One of them was Damodar Thakkur, author of *Sangramsahityavivekdipika* and *Divyanirnay* and elder brother of Mahesh Thakkur, the renowned scholar who was part of first Durgawati's and then Akbar's court. From all accounts, Sangram Shah's court had both scholarly depth and administrative acumen thanks to able ministers such as Diwan Bhoj Kayath and Madhav, grandson of Sarve Pathak, who was prime minister to Yadavrai, founder of the dynasty. Bhoj Kayath, in fact, continued in service for more than three decades. According to Abul Fazl, he was the senior noble appointed by Bir Narayan to conduct the jauhar that claimed the lives of all the women left behind in the fort of Chauragarh when the prince went out on his final battle with Asaf Khan.

The thirty-plus years of stability that Sangram Shah ensured saw a number of temples and forts being built—an expensive proposition possible only if a kingdom could afford it. In fact, Sangram Shah is credited with building some of the most iconic structures in and around Gondwana. Apart from the Sangram Sagar lake and Bajnamath Temple mentioned earlier, this list includes the fortress of Chauragarh which, says Sleeman,

> from the brow of the range of hills that form its southern boundary, still overlooks the valley of the Nerbudda . . . [and] he [Sangram Shah] continued himself to reside in the palace Madan Mahal, a part of which still stands on the hill near Garha, and overlooks the great reservoir and temple in which he is believed to have offered up to the god of truth so agreeable a sacrifice in the blood of a base assassin.[15]

Modern historians like Suresh Mishra believe that the iconic Madan Mahal too was built by Sangram Shah.

Despite Abul Fazl's frequent tut-tutting about Sangram Shah and the way he captured the throne, the truth is Amhandas was both a capable and an unusual ruler. How unusual becomes clear from a story about one of his coins. In 1937, the British Museum recorded several donations of antique Indian coins from individual collectors, many of whom were civilians of the Raj. Among hoards of Mughal,

Kalachuri, Chola and Chalukya coins was one 'unique' specimen. Donated by a Robert Sutcliffe, this gold coin from Garha Mandla had on its obverse a very curious legend: 'Pulastavamsa Sri Sangrama Sahi Samvat 1600'.[16] Dated around 1543, this rare coin references another aspect of Sangram Shah—a king who unapologetically and proudly wore his Gond antecedents on his coinage, linking his lineage to Ravan's grandfather, the sage Pulatasya, in a time-honoured tribal tradition. This caste confidence and the military reputation that backed it up are also the reason why Dalpati could marry Durgawati despite the reservations of her Rajput father. That their union is only the second Gond–Rajput marriage in the dynasty's history is also telling.

Today, popular imagination has largely forgotten Sangram Shah. Even Gond folk songs don't mention him that often. The ones that do hauntingly highlight how the footprints of this mighty monarch have been erased by the caprice of time. '*Kahan gaye Raja Amhan, ban ki rovay chiroya?*' ('The birds of the forest cry in despair, where did Raja Amhan go?') laments a rare folk elegy, its simple verse capturing the fate that history reserved for this monarch. And if the songs have forgotten, so have the stones. Apart from the Bajnamath Temple and Sangram Sagar lake in Jabalpur city and a small village called Singrampur a half-hour ride away, not too many footprints of this once-powerful king remain in the kingdom he called his own.

That's because another monarch—more honourable, more heroic and more memorable—has taken his place. Ironically, it was neither his heir nor the spare that took

Sangram Shah's legacy forward and left an everlasting imprint on history. The monarch who did so was the Chandel princess who married into his family, his daughter-in-law Rani Durgawati.

4

Love and Longing

'*Nirjitya bhuupal samuuha maajou Durgaavati kaamavati jahaar*'

(He snatched away Durgawati who was full of desire)

—Rupnath Jha, 'Gadhesh Nrpa Varnim'

It was a balmy winter evening in the beginning of the year 1542. A beautiful Rajput princess was doing what teenage girls like to do, then as now—dreaming about a dashing young man. At eighteen years of age, Chandela princess Durgawati of Rath Mahoba was already a celebrated beauty. A seventeenth-century Mughal miniature (currently on display in Government Museum, Chennai) highlights her features— big eyes, noble brow, dainty nose, small rosebud mouth and a determined chin. Petite and pleasingly proportioned, she strikes an unusually feminine pose, holding a flower in one hand. One look at the painting is enough to understand why her grace and charm were mentioned over and over again, even by her adversaries. Add to them her impeccable lineage as the scion of one of the oldest Rajput bloodlines in the region as well as her reputation as a keen horse rider and a crack shot, and it becomes obvious why she was considered quite the catch.

Nothing much is known about Durgawati's childhood and adolescence, and even historical fiction accounts begin the story with her teenage romance. According to a recently discovered horoscope of the queen, she was born on 5 October 1524.[1] Durgawati had a sister called Kamlawati, though it is not known whether she was a younger or older sibling. Even though her patrimony—the tiny kingdom of Rath Mahoba ruled by her father Shalivahan/Salbahan—was nothing to write home about, Durgawati's accomplishments merited a *swayamvar*, the ancient Hindu ritual by which royal brides chose their own husband from a collection of guests invited to the event. But the trouble was, Durgawati was in love with a man who was neither Rajput nor a candidate approved by her father.

Rath and Mahoba can now be located in UP's Hamirpur district. Just 80 km to its south was the Gond kingdom of Garha Katanga with its capital in Singorgarh, currently located in Singrampur village of Damoh district, 45 km from Jabalpur city. This land was ruled by Raj Gond king Sangram Shah, whose older son and heir Dalpati/Dalpat Shah was the man Durgawati had lost her heart to.

Where and how did the young princess meet her prince charming? There are various local tales that have been quoted by both historians and writers. Well-known litterateur Vrindavan Lal Varma, author of the 1960s cult classic *Maharani Durgawati*, shows the two lovers meeting first at the Mania Devi temple in Mahoba and later on a return-invite hunt near Kalinjar Fort. This hunt-romance, though comes with a confusing thread. Historians like R.V. Russel and Rai Bahadur Hiralal say that it was 'Chandel Raja Keerat Singh' who was out 'hunting at Maniagarh with the Gond Raja of Garha Mandla'.[2] Given that Keerat Singh is often confused as Durgawati's father, this reference may be apocryphal. But there is no doubt the lovers met in secret, and out of such clandestine meetings was born a love story that continues to live on in bard song to this day. Local folk traditions still remember this romance as much as the queen's final sacrifice. The song *Maa Veerangana Durgawati Maharani* by Gond folk singer Ramkumar Dhruva, for example, talks of both incidents one after the other. '*Garh Mandla ke Dalpati Raja preme piyari lagayi/ Bade pratapi raja they weh Durga se shaadi rachayi/Mughalo se woh ladi larai kabhi har na mani/ lartay lartay Narai Nala pahuch gayee*' ('Garha Mandla's Dalpati Raja was madly in love/He was a powerful king and he married Durga/She fought against the Mughals and refused to give up/She reached Narai Nala still fighting off the threat'). Indeed, every folk tradition about Durgawati mentions *coeur et courage* in the same breath. In folk memory, the Gond queen is remembered both for love and war.

Even as she dreamt of her prince charming, the teenage Durgawati knew how impossible their love was. As a Rajput and a princess, she understood only too well what was expected of her. She had to choose her husband from among the guests approved and invited by her father. Unfortunately, she also knew that the man she really wanted to marry would certainly not be invited to the swayamvar.

Although good-looking, courageous and the crown prince of a powerful neighbouring kingdom, Dalpati or Dalpat Shah was Gond, not Rajput. His father Sangram Shah had approved the match, but Shalivahan was not interested.

Sleeman describes the situation in his inimitable style.

> Overtures had been made for a union between Dulput Sa [Dalpati Shah] and Durghoutee [Durgawati], the daughter of the raja of Mahoba, who was much celebrated for her singular beauty; but the proposal was rejected on the ground of a previous engagement, and some inferiority of caste on the part of the Gurha family.[3]

Parental disapproval notwithstanding, there was good reason for Durgawati to be smitten. The Gond crown prince was an exceptionally good-looking man, and he was the scion of what was then the largest and most powerful kingdom in central India. While royal panegyrics are never short of hyperbole, in the case of Dalpati and Durgawati, their beauty is something all chroniclers, contemporary and otherwise, invariably mention. In contemporary references, literary chronicles and bard song, Dalpati Shah is as celebrated for his looks as Durgawati herself. Anant Dixit, a sixteenth-century poet who was Dalpati Shah's contemporary, says the Gond prince was '*Madan sadrisha roop*' or as handsome as Madan, the god of love himself. He mentions this while describing Dalpati and Durga in the *Gadhesh Nrpa Varnan Samagrah Slokah*, an anthology of Sanskrit poems compiled in the sixteenth century. Durgawati is similarly called '*sundari*'. Sleeman describes Dalpati Shah's 'appearance' with

characteristic romantic flourish. 'Dulput Sa (Dalpati Shah),'
he writes, 'was a man of uncommonly fine appearance and
this, added to the celebrity of his father's name and extent of
his dominion, made Durghoutee (Durgawati) as desirous as
himself for the union.'[4]

For his part, Dalpati would have undoubtedly heard of the
feisty Chandel princess whose beauty nearly every contemporary
chronicler talked about, right from Abul Fazl to Badauni and
Ferishta to Anant Dixit. Indeed, a century after her death, the
Ramnagar inscription on Raj Gond genealogy remembered
Durgawati as the very embodiment of Goddess Lakshmi. 'His
[Dalpati Shah] consort Durgawati was as prosperity itself to
the fortunes of petitioners, beautiful as the image of virtue, the
boundary of the good fortune of this earth.'[5] Clearly, Dalpati
and Durga made a fine couple indeed.

Because of Shalivahan's refusal to accept a Raj Gond son-
in-law, the two lovers devised a plan to elope. Literary sources
and folk traditions say Durgawati sent word to her prince to
come and get her. Although this would have been unusual in
the strictly regimented medieval world she inhabited, in using
the age-old tradition of *harana vivah* (where the bride invites
a champion to fight for her hand), the princess was merely
taking a cue from the option used by other gutsy women
before her like Subhadra and Rukmini in the Mahabharat
and Sanyogita in the twelfth century.

There are two versions of what happened, both equally
romantic. According to Sleeman, Dalpati

> was by her [Durgawati] given to understand, that she must
> be relinquished or taken by force, since the difference

of caste would of itself be otherwise an insurmountable
obstacle. He marched with all the troops he could
assemble, met those of her father and his rival, gained a
victory, and brought off Durghoutee [Durgawati] as the
prize to the fort of Singorgurh.[6]

For its part, the *Gadhesh Nrpa Varnan Samagrah Slokah* also
documents similar, if not exact, details about this Gond–
Rajput love story. According to a particular sloka by Anant
Dixit, Dalpati had heard from a *bipra* or priest that Durgawati
was in love with him. So he took his father's permission to
attend her swayamvar with a group of his choicest men.
With great courage, Dalpati defeated all the other kings who
challenged his claim to Durga's hand and rode away with her.

'*Shrutvaa   vipramukhatswayamvaravare   svaakarshan
prematastaataajyaa/Parilakshya yo hi gatavaansatsainyatadwiprayuk/
Advrishtaashvatithou yute Dalapatinirmarthya svaarodhakaanu/
Shri Chandelasutaa jahaar balavaan Durgavati shrimatiim.*'

Another literary source, the eighteenth-century poem
'Gadhesh Nrpa Varnim' by poet Rupnath Jha also describes
the swayamvar and the elopement: '*Svayamvaro yo gatavaan
sasayinyo nripa vara yatra samaagataa vai/Nirjitya bhuupal
samuuha maajou Durgaavati kaamavati jahaar*' ('Dalpati
Shah accompanied by his army went for the swayamvara
where had also assembled the best of the kings; there having
utterly defeated in battle the group of kings he snatched away
Durgawati who was full of desire').[7]

Local chroniclers mention a slightly different version
of the story, which has been documented by historian
G.V. Bhave. 'To know the antecedents of the marriage we have

to take the help of local chroniclers who affirm that Dalpati and Durgawati were in love with each other, each being extraordinarily charming by form and figure,' writes Bhave.

> Durgawati at last wrote a letter to her lover at Singor Gadh that she had seen him in her dream and that if he really loved her, he should go to Mahoba on the Vasant Panchami day when her parents usually went out to visit the temple of Durga situated outside town. Dalpati accordingly took with him a force of 12,000 soldiers and carried away his object of love to Singor Gadh where the marriage was performed with due rites.[8]

Clearly, whether he fought off his challengers at the swayamvar or swept in and carried his bride away in a pre-planned raid, Dalpati would have caused quite a flutter with his daredevilry. But the Gond crown prince could afford to do something quite so reckless because he was confident both of his lady's love and of his kingdom's military superiority over Mahoba. Bhave says that the fact that the slokas in *Gadhesh Nrpa Varnan Samagrah Slokah* clearly mention that Dalpati took his father's permission before eloping with Durgawati shows

> that his father Sangram Shah had his full consent in this heroic mischief on the part of Dalpati. No doubt the example of Prithviraj and Sanyogita was brilliantly running before them but that alone was not enough. The fact that Dalpati's illustrious father Sangram Shah had perhaps been widely known for his extensive power and

that Dalpati was himself conscious of his firm position
must have encouraged him to take this extra bold step.[9]

Abul Fazl gives another angle to the story, which shows that
when it comes to territory and military might, Shalivahan
was really no match for the Raj Gonds. In the *Akbarnama*,
Abul Fazl writes that Shalivahan was compelled to marry his
daughter to Dalpati Shah even though in terms of lineage,
the Raj Gonds were no match for the Chandelas. This is
because Shalivahan's 'circumstance' was a bit precarious,
and he basically did not have a choice. Shalivahan, wrote
Abul Fazl, gave Durgawati 'in marriage to Dalpat [Dalpati],
the son of Amhan Das [Sangram Shah]. Though he was not
of a good family yet as he was wealthy and Rajah Shalivahan
was in bad circumstances, the latter was compelled to make
this alliance.'[10]

     To emphasize just how mismatched the couple were,
Abul Fazl goes ahead and sprinkles a fair bit of salacious gossip
about Dalpati's lineage, suggesting in a decidedly nudge-
nudge wink-wink manner that the crown prince was not quite
to the manor born. 'There was a report that Sangram had no
son and that he requested Gobind Das Kachwaha, who was
his servant, to allow his pregnant wife to be delivered in the
former's harem,' writes Abul Fazl.

     If there was a daughter, Gobind Das would have her, and
     if there was a son, Sangram would take him as his. No one
     was to be told of this. Gobind Das obeyed the order, and
     when his wife was delivered of a son the Rajah took him

as his own. He gave him the name of Dalpat, and Rani
Durgawati was given in marriage to him.[11]

It is another matter that Sangram Shah did have another son,
Chandra Shah, who ultimately inherited the kingdom after
the death of Durgawati and her son. That curious snippet
about Dalpati Shah comes on the heels of more shame and
scandal revelations from Abul Fazl, this time about Amhandas
or Sangram Shah himself. As mentioned in the earlier chapter,
Fazl is positively scathing about Amhandas, imputing to him
all manner of treachery, including patricide.

Dark stuff indeed. But even if we discount all these
blood-curling titbits, the union of Dalpati and Durgawati
was certainly an unusual one, no matter what Abul Fazl may
say about Shalivahan's compulsions. How unusual becomes
clear when we see how few such marriages are documented
by history or in local bard song. Apart from Dalpati and
Durgawati, only one more celebrated Gond–Rajput couple
crops up in folklore—Gond princess Ratnavali, who married
the Rajput adventurer Yadu Rai/Yadav Rai, the man who
inherited his father-in-law's kingdom and founded the Raj
Gond dynasty. In his seminal book *The Gond and Bhumia of
Eastern Mandla*, Stephen Fuchs writes:

> During the time when the Gond spread all over
> Gondwana . . . they must also have come in close contact
> with the Rajputs . . . Though the Gond themselves may
> not have been averse to intermarriage . . . these non-
> tribals were barred by their caste rules from forming
> marital unions with the Gonds on a large scale . . . only

some chiefs of the Gond were able to marry into a Rajput family. Thus the Gond Raja Dalpati Shah married the Rajput princess Durgawati.[12]

While Dalpati may not have been quite the suitable boy that King Shalivahan was hoping to marry his daughter to, Durgawati's own lineage too was illustrious mostly by association. Indeed the most well-known sixteenth-century Chandel king from central India that history remembers is not Shalivahan, but Keerat Singh, who was the lord of the Kalinjar Fort and was also Sher Shah Suri's contemporary. Sher Shah in fact lost his life in an expedition to storm Kalinjar Fort, where a blast backfired and killed him.

The fact that the two Chandel monarchs were contemporaries and ruled kingdoms close to each other has led to considerable confusion about the name of the Rajput king who was, in fact, Durgawati's father—is it Shalivahan as Abul Fazl, mentions or is it Keerat Singh? Earlier historians like Vincent Smith, Alexander Cunningham and Keshab Chandra Mishra maintained that the Kalinjar overlord Keerat Singh was also Durgawati's father. But modern historians say that as a contemporary source, the *Akbarnama*'s account should be accepted as authentic. In other words: Shalivahan and Keerat Singh were two different kings from the Chandela line. Eminent historian from Bhopal Dr Suresh Mishra, an authority on the kingdom of Garha Mandla/Garha Katanga in general and Rani Durgawati in particular, has an explanation about why this confusion over the name of Durgawati's father has been so pernicious. 'It seems these historians have suggested this connection between Shalivahan and Keerat Singh in an effort to link Durgawati's linage with the main Chandela line whereas in reality her father was an insignificant overlord who ruled Rath Mahoba,' says Dr Mishra. According to him, there is a very good reason why this confusion is intrinsically linked to the history of Bundelkhand itself. For two centuries before Shalivahan, Bundelkhand was controlled by Chandela kings, and Mahoba was their capital right up until the twelfth century. The capital moved from Mahoba to Kalinjar only in the early thirteenth century after the Chandelas were defeated by Qutubuddin Aibak. 'The main Chandela line continued in Kalinjar through the fifteenth century and early sixteenth century even as a branch line ruled in Rath Mahoba,' says Dr Mishra. 'History does not tell us if there was any connection between Sher Shah Suri, his contemporary Chandela Raja Keerat Singh and the Rath Mahoba ruler Shalivahan who was Durgawati's father.' Clearly, the fate of the Kalinjar Fort and the final battle that cost Sher Shah Suri his life impacted Durgawati and Dalpati Shah only indirectly, creating a power vacuum in the region that substantially altered the military equations in central India and earned local sovereigns some much-needed elbow room. Indeed, the way contemporary historians describe the fall of Kalinjar shows how hard-fought this elbow room was.

According to the *Tarikh-i-Sher Shahi*, written by Afghan historian Abbas Khan Sarwani in the mid-sixteenth century at the behest of Mughal Emperor Akbar, the reason why Sher Shah attacked Kalinjar in the first place was not because of its strategic importance but because of his interest in a beautiful *patar* or dancing girl in Keerat Singh's seraglio. 'The motives behind the capture of the fort lay in the fact that there was a

dancing slave girl in the harem of Keerat Singh about whom
Sher Khan had heard a lot of praise,' writes Sarwani. 'He had
therefore a desire to capture her in any way. If he would seize
the fort by force, Raja Keerat Singh would certainly cause
jauhar and thus burn the slave girl.'[13] This salacious twist
apart, the real reason why Sher Shah attacked Kalinjar may
have had to do with the power struggle between the Afghans
and the Mughals. Some of the more powerful kings in this
region had become embroiled in this power tussle, attracting
the military attention of first Sher Shah Suri and later Akbar.
Raja Vir Bhanu of Rewa, for example, was very friendly with
Humayun and had helped him escape to Agra after the defeat
at Chausa. So Sher Shah's expedition was intended to crush
Raja Vir Bhanu as well as other independent kingdoms in the
region that he saw as hostile to his interests. Vir Bhanu took
refuge in Kalinjar and thus brought Sher Shah to its gates.

Sarwani's account also completely glosses over the fact
that the resistance Sher Shah faced in this expedition was
tough enough for him to try some out-of-the-box ideas,
which he then goes on to describe. For one, he decided to
surround the fort with a high rampart so as to use his snipers
to pick off the people behind its walls. 'In a short time, he
raised the entrenchment to such a height that the fort of
Kalinjar came to be overtopped,' writes Sarwani. 'The people
who moved in the streets and houses became visible from the
tops of the entrenchments. Those Hindus who were found
moving in the streets and houses were shot with arrows and
guns by the Afghans.' This is in keeping with Sarwani's firm
belief that Sher Shah's attack on Kalinjar was part of a jihad
at the insistence of his religious advisors. Sher Shah's final

gambit, however, backfired, quite literally, when he ordered some bombardments on the fort. 'When the men became engaged in shooting the rockets, a rocket struck against the fort and exploded,' writes Sarwani. 'The rocket which broke forth rebounded and fell at the place where rockets had been lying in large numbers.' The resultant explosion burnt Sher Shah very badly. He died on 22 May 1545.

While this bloody battle shook the entire region and would have doubtless been keenly followed by the Raj Gond court, Durgawati and Dalpati were wrapped up in their own bubble of happiness during this time. This was the year that the royal couple were blessed with a baby boy, Bir Narayan. Durgawati was already the Gond queen of Garha Katanga because, just two years before, Dalpati Shah had ascended the throne after the death of his father. The kingdom was brimming over with peace and possibility. In the palace, there was harmony not only between the royal couple but also between Sangram Shah's two wives—Padmavati (Dalpati's mother) and Sumati—and his two sons Dalpati and his younger brother Chandra. Sher Shah's death allowed the local monarchs in central India to flex their muscles and consolidate their sovereignty. For the first time in nearly 300 years, Delhi was too far away to be a worry for the Raj Gonds. At least for the moment.

5

End of the Idyll: Happiness and Heartbreak

'Dalapati nrpati preyasi kalpavallih ksonyam anya vadanyavadhir amalaguna bhati Durgavatiha'

(Durgawati, the beloved of King Dalapati, is the epitome of benevolence and virtue)

—Samayalok

Sher Shah's sudden death in the battle of Kalinjar left his central Indian agenda in disarray. His successors were not strong enough to follow through his military plans and were too focused on the shenanigans of their own nobles to bother very much. Dalpati, and by extension Garha—one of the most prosperous kingdoms in central India at the time—benefited from this political breathing space. What also helped Dalpati was his father's formidable reputation, both in derring-do and diplomacy. His neighbours largely minded their own business, allowing the newly crowned Raj Gond monarch to consolidate his rule. Take the Baghel kingdom of Rewa to the north-east of Garha. Vir Bhanu had passed away, and his son Raja Ram Chand/Ram Chandra was on the throne when Dalpati became king. Like his father, Dalpati maintained cordial relations with his Baghel neighbours, with whom he shared a long common border. As a result, there are no reports of any border skirmishes between these two powerful kingdoms, either during Dalpati's time or later when Durgawati was in charge. (Though, as we shall see later on, Ram Chandra's intransigence in the face of Mughal hostility did cost him his battle with Asaf Khan and the fall of Panna/Rewa brought the rampaging imperial army right up to Durgawati's doorstep.) In a sense, the battle of Kalinjar was a boon for Dalpati and Durgawati because it gave them what all newly-weds dream of—the chance to spend some quality couple time with each other without political or military disruptions and distractions. With new responsibilities both as monarchs and parents, this period of peace was perfect for the newly anointed king and queen of Garha. All through these years, Durgawati's family life was almost picture-perfect. The Gonds loved their new queen right from the beginning—indeed, when Dalpati and Durgawati galloped away from Mahoba to Singorgarh, all of Garha cheered for the much-in-love couple. The old king Sangram Shah had already blessed the union by allowing his son and heir to undertake the risky elopement, and the romance became part of both folk as well literary lore. In fact, a collection of slokas discovered by Pandit Vasudevrao Golwalkar and later translated by G.B. Bhave in the 1940s describe how popular sentiment viewed this love story: '*Abdeshta shwatitho yute Dalpati nirmathya swarodhakaan/*

Sri Chandelasutam jahar balvan Durgavatim srimatim' ('The brave Dalpati defeated all his rivals and snatched away his prize—the Chandel princess Srimati Durgawati'). For the young and handsome Gond crown prince, this act of chivalry was a real feather in his cap. It added to his charisma and earned him a reputation for near-mythical gallantry. The Gonds welcomed the feisty new crown princess into their hearts, singing paeans to her beauty, virtue and good fortune. They knew their prince had secured an excellent match for himself, both in terms of looks as well as in terms of lineage. The Ramnagar inscription shows just how chuffed they were about his choice of consort: '*Samriddhireva swarupini purnyaparamparaiva sawbhagyasimaiva vasundharaya Durgawati tasya babhuvapatni*' ('Durgawati was as prosperity herself, beautiful as the image of virtue, the very boundary of good fortune on earth').[1]

The couple would have had a lavish wedding befitting the crown prince of a prosperous and powerful kingdom. There is some slight confusion regarding the actual wedding date. While some historians say the elopement happened in 1542, other sources (including the *Gadhesh Nrpa Varnam*) fix the date on Vasant Panchami, Sunday, 2 January 1541. The wedding happened two days later on Vasant Saptami, 4 January. There are no contemporary descriptions of the event, but royal weddings described in Gond folk tales give us some clues. In the story of Lohabandha Raja, a Pradhan folk tale from Balaghat, Gond Raja Karaikuar is shown marrying princess Urmal Karo in a glittering ceremony. The queen's trousseau is rich and elaborate: Her 'clothes were of gold, a skirt from the south, a jacket from the east, her anklets were from Raj Ratan, her bangles were of Indrajot, her toe rings came from Rai Bhajan. The bun of her hair was worth a lakh and a quarter of rupees, her necklace was worth 9 lakhs'. As for the groom, he is no less elaborately attired: 'The Raja's shawl was worth a lakh-and-a-quarter rupees, his coat was worth 9 lakhs. His turban was worth 32 lakhs and he had a necklace of elephant pearls.'[2] The story goes on to detail the ceremony itself: 'The wedding took 15 days. The colours of the silken booth were red, pink, white, grey and purple', and the dowry was '12 strings of goats' and '12 strings of sheep. Nuts and sweets were given to everyone. There were sweet laddus. The chief dish was rice with pulse of Urad and Moong. When the party left, 60 *kahar* were employed to carry their litters'. After travelling for eight days and nine nights, they got home and had the 'perambulation ceremony' and 'all the people were invited'.

Gond folk tales give us a glimpse of the way popular imagination has remembered the history of the region. Gond kings and queens, including Dalpati and Durgawati, often pop up in these simple stories. The Lohabandha legend makes no mention of Rani Durgawati or her husband Dalpati Shah. But its description of royal nuptials may well reflect a fragment of collective memory—full of colourful decorations, lavish feasts and weeks-long celebrations and not unlike the kind of wedding that Sangram Shah would have organized for the crown prince and princess.

The old king's wedding gift to the new bride was both generous and prophetic. According to local lore documented by Jabalpur-based historian Dr Shashi Saraf, Durgawati's first public appearance after the wedding was when she touched her father-in-law's feet, and he gifted her a huge piece of land in return. She would go on to use a large parcel from this land to construct a lake that still bears her name—Ranital. To this day, this tank stands as a reminder of Durgawati's laudable focus on public good all through her reign. As Sleeman said about her: 'She built the great reservoir which lies close to Jabalpur and is called after her Rani Talao or Queen's Pond and many other highly useful works were formed by her about Garha.'[3]

The Ranital was just the first in a long line of lakes and tanks that the queen sponsored, to honour members of her family as well as important officials in her court. Next to Ranital, for example, is the smaller lake Cherital, built with donations from her lady-in-waiting, and a tank facing the Maha Lakshmi Temple was built to honour her diwan Adhar Kayastha and was called Adhartal. Local lore also credits her with honouring her general or Senapati Chakraman with a lake named Mantal in Jabalpur, which is now called Hanumantal. Another general, the Miyana Afghan Bukhari Rumi, says Saraf, was honoured with a water body called Bukharital, which is now called Ukhrital. In time, Durgawati would come to be known as the lady of the lakes (*tal talab Rani*), with water bodies named after not just her, but her son (Balsagar) and even her favourite elephant Sarman (Hathital). Her kingdom Garha was known as the land of *bhavan tal, chausath talayian* (fifty-two big tanks and sixty-four small ponds).

Of course, much of this would come later. For the moment, the crown princess was busy with happy domesticity, even though this role turned out to be a very short-lived one for her. Tragedy struck when Sangram Shah passed away in 1543, leaving Dalpati in charge of the realm. There is no record of any dispute regarding the throne, and from all accounts the coronation ceremony went ahead without any hiccups. If younger brother Chandra Shah resented Dalpati's pre-eminence, he held his tongue, and the cordiality among family members continued as before.

Sangram Shah used to live in Madan Mahal, the precariously perched mini fort that is now Jabalpur's most iconic historical calling card. Because of its height, it offered an excellent view of the terrain all around and doubled up as a watch tower as well. After Dalpati became king, however, he moved his capital from Garha to Singorgarh. Currently, the crumbling fort of Singorgarh lies a very picturesque, forty-five-minute drive out of Jabalpur, the still reasonably thick forest cover giving an indication of just how inaccessible it must have been nearly five centuries ago. Dalpati found this remoteness ideal and refurbished the fort to make it habitable for the royal family. The *Gadhesh Nrpa Sangraha Slokah* mentions this saying: '*Nrpa Dalapati Shahi: Sinhadurgay stithiyarth*' ('King Dalpati Shah decided to stay at Sinha durg or Singorgarh').

There are several theories about how Singorgarh Fort got its name. The Tharraka sati inscription that references Amandas Deo or Sangram Shah also says that the village and adjoining areas were part of the Srigarh Gatiri Vishaya Durg. Could Singorgarh be a derivation of Srigarh Durg? A later ruler could have imposed his name on this variant and called it Gajsingh Durg, which is how an inscription found in the fort actually refers to the structure. Singorgarh Fort included around 350 villages, though this region was not, at that time, a heavily populated part of Gondwana.[4] This scenic if secluded place is where Dalpati and Durgawati moved in and watched the political scenario around them change with blink-and-miss rapidity.

Despite the precaution of moving to a more remote fort for protection, Dalpati did face one skirmish during his rule. The *Gadhesh* mentions a siege invasion by the Ruhilla Nawab Umar Khan: '*Balay Umar Khano bhunna vabo Ruhilla/ Varmati sachivo sthyadhar kayasth dheerah*' ('The Ruhilla Nawab Umar Khan encircled the Singorgarh fort like a bangle but thanks to the quick thinking of minister Adhar Kayastha, this attack was repulsed'). This reference is significant for two reasons—first, the siege was clearly not a long-drawn affair and was quickly and effectively repulsed, which explains why it is not mentioned by other contemporary sources; second, it shows that Adhar Kayastha, who was a key official during Durgawati's reign as well, was already a trusted minister when Dalpati was on the throne. Durgawati probably depended on him so much—right till the end when she faced defeat and death, as we shall see—because he was chosen by her husband and had already proved his worth while working for Dalpati.

Dalpati and Durgawati were lucky to enjoy several years of blissful married life. This period of tranquillity allowed the rani to concentrate on her duties as queen and mother, devoting her time to puja, temple building and other sacred duties. The *Prastab Ratnakar*, a Sanskrit book commissioned by Durgawati and written in 1557 for prince Bir Narayan by his tutor Pandit Haridas, gives us some clues about the rites and rituals that governed royal life.

'*Saumay budho guro shukhray soumyavarah shubhapradah*',
says the book. The prince is being instructed that Mondays,
Wednesdays, Thursdays and Fridays are the right days to
consecrate a deity in a temple. And which are the auspicious
months when this can be done? The *Prastab Ratnakar* lays
out the calendar: '*Chaitray va phalgunay chaiva jaishthay va
madhavay tatha/ Maghay cha sarvativanam pratishtha sarvada
bhaveth*', which means the months of Chaitra (March–April),
Phalgun (February–March), Jaishtha (May–June), Vaisakh
(April–May) and Magh (January–February) are ideal for
consecrating a temple. Given that Durgawati is associated
with a number of temples from the Sharada Mata Mandir
near Madan Mahal to the Barman Ghat Shiva Temple in
Narsinghpur district, the slokas give an idea of how busy her
schedule would have been.

Her husband too would have had similar responsibilities,
conducting elaborate fire sacrifices on auspicious occasions
and offering patronage to scholars and donations to those in
need. The *Gadhesh Nrpa Varnam*'s description of him gives
us an idea of how much of Dalpati's reputation, which lasted
a good century and a half despite his short rule, depended
on his sacred duties: '*Vividhavibha vayukto yagnya karta
badanyah/kulkamaldineshah kirtijyo vatrkeshah*' ('He was a
performer of sacrifices of different kinds and was a patron
of renown; he was the sun for the lotus of his own family').[5]

Beyond devotion, the queen also focused attention on
charitable work, which quickly earned her a reputation
for generosity worthy of panegyric hyperbole. 'There are
stories current in Hindustan of her feasts and her frays,' says
Abul Fazl, grudgingly acknowledging her popularity in the

Akbarnama. Mandla historian Pandit Ganesh Dutt Pathak quoted manuscripts in his collection to say that Durgawati once donated an eye-popping one crore gold coins in charity. Another example of her love of literature and eagerness to patronize poetry in her court comes out in a rare sloka from a handwritten manuscript unearthed by Pathak more than sixty years ago. It goes thus: '*Diyatam diggajashchet sakal vasumati yati patalamulam/Vahashchet saptasapteh trijagat bhibhaveth andhakarsthamobhih/ Swarnadi diyate chet kathamvanitale sanchareyuh Surendrah/Ki datwam preyshaniam kaviriti hridaye muncha Durgay vishadam.*' Loosely translated, it says that Queen Durgawati was concerned about what gifts to offer a poet who was leaving her court. If she offered elephants, the earth would descend to Patal Lok because the elephants were holding it aloft. If she offered horses, the Sun God would not be able to drive his chariot across the sky. If she offered gold, the Sumeru hoard of Goddess Devi would be depleted. So, what should the queen offer a man who writes such exquisite poetry?

This large-heartedness is a quality that Durgawati shared with her husband, who peppered his short seven-year-rule with some generous grants that cut across religious lines. On the one hand, Dalpati Shah donated the Ramangara village to a Brahmin pujari of a local Radha Krishna temple in Rampur. The Brahmin families of Ramangara to this day say that their kinsmen preserved the copperplate inscription of the land grant that gave them rights over the village.[6] On the other hand, he also made donations to a holy man called Sri Baba Kapur Sahib, who was either a Kabirpanthi (Kabir's follower) or a Sufi saint.[7] According to a copperplate inscription discovered in Jabalpur, the king donated two villages, Kuda and Kachanari, and ordered every household therein to contribute a half-price coin for the upkeep of the holy man.

Dalpati's reign of ripple-less peace comes with a charming back story. According to local lore, the crown prince had promised his mother Queen Padmavati that he would stay away from the kind of bloodlust that tainted his father's rise to power. Before riding off to claim his love, the prince, says the popular story, laid down his arms at his mother's feet and promised her he would focus on peace and not war.[8] From all accounts, he stuck to that promise (even if the back story is an apocryphal one) and thus managed to steer outside Sher Shah's successor Islam Shah Suri's radar. That does not mean he was either weak or indecisive. There are examples of him shuffling his jagirdars in an attempt to quell local rebellion. According to the Bilaspur Gazetteer of 1910,[9] the Lodhi chieftain of Pandaria, who owed allegiance to the king of Garha Mandla, rebelled in 1546. He was overthrown and the zamindari handed over to a Raj Gond called Sham Chand, who was the fourteenth generation ancestor of the zamindar in charge of Pandaria in 1910. The Gazetteer says this reshuffle was done with the consent of the local feudatory raja. 'With the consent of the Raja of Lanji, Sham Chand was confirmed in his possession of Pandaria which was then known as Mukutpur Partabgarh,' said the Gazetteer. Given that Abul Fazl also mentions the raja of Lanji as one of the Raj Gond feudatories and that Dalpati was most certainly on the throne in 1546, this event must have happened during his reign.

For Durgawati, the tranquillity of the times also meant that, every now and then, she could squeeze time out for her favourite pastime—shikar. And it is on a tiger hunt that she forged a bond of a lifetime with her favourite mount, the elephant Sarman. According to Mandla historian Ram Bharosh Agarwal of the Gondi Public Trust, this loyal and fearsome animal was presented to her near Bhawartal, which used to be a lake but is now a sprawling, well-maintained public garden featuring, appropriately enough, a statue of Durgawati astride Sarman. Agarwal relates several charming tales about Sarman that were part of the local lore even sixty years ago, when he was writing his book on the Raj Gond dynasty. One such story is about why Durgawati forged such a close bond with Sarman. The queen was a keen hunter, and she loved to go on tiger hunts in Gondwana's thick forests. Abul Fazl records her reputation as a crack shot and shikari in the *Akbarnama*: 'She was a good shot with gun and arrow, and continually went a-hunting, and shot animals of the chase with her gun,' he wrote. 'It was her custom that whenever she heard that a tiger had made his appearance, she did not drink water till she had shot him.'[10] Durgawati's renown as a shikari is so well-entrenched that a panel sculpture in a temple in Madhupuri in Mandla district shows her killing a tiger. According to Agarwal, this panel was installed by Madhukar Shah, son of Chandra Shah, who ruled just a decade-and-a-half after Durgawati. While some historians now maintain that these temple panels depict generic Gond hunts rather than a particular queen, that local lore would connect the Gond Rani with a hunt-sculpture shows that her reputation as a shikari was well-established indeed.

On one such tiger hunt, the queen decided to take her new elephant Sarman with her. During the course of the hunt, even as Durga was stalking the tiger on elephant back, it turned around and attacked her instead, badly scratching the elephant's hind quarter. Normally, an injured elephant is blinded by pain and runs amok, trampling everyone and everything underfoot. But not Sarman. 'The elephant was very badly injured by the tiger's attack but it still managed to escape from the jungle carrying the queen back to safety,' says Shashi Saraf. 'Durgawati never forgot this loyalty and from then on, she seldom rode any other mount. She also built the Hathital tank in Sarman's honour.' Over the years, Sarman became as much a son to her as the infant Bir Narayan. In the morning, when she sat down for her puja, the elephant would carry in a pitcher full of water from the holy Narmada and place it before her for the rituals.[11]

Of course, Sarman was not the only elephant in the queen's extensive stable and she, so the legend goes, also had a rare white elephant. Indeed, contemporary literary work *Durgawati Gajavarnam* mentions her formidable line-up of elephants, and there are quite a few contemporary anecdotes that tie Durgawati to these majestic beasts. One of them concerns a promising if hot-headed scholar called Raghunandan Rai, who was the most favoured student of Pandit Mahesh Thakkur. Maithil Brahmin Mahesh Thakkur and his brother Damodar Thakkur had been invited to settle down in Garha by Sangram Shah. In time, Mahesh Thakkur became a much-venerated presence in Garha and was also appointed the Raj Purohit by Dalpati Shah. Incidentally, Thakkur was also Diwan Adhar Kayastha's *diksha* guru. Both

Dalpati and Durgawati were devoted to him and would listen to his discourse on the Puranas every day. The story goes that one day, Thakkur could not attend to his duties and sent his favourite student instead. Raghunandan Rai, in an effort to impress his royal patrons, tried to make the discussion more detailed than usual, but his verbosity had the opposite effect. Durgawati was unhappy with the replacement, and this led to a tiff between her and Raghunandan, who left in a huff for Bastar. He then so impressed the king of Bastar that he received seven elephants as reward. Rai promptly donated one of these to Durgawati in an act of revenge generosity and gave the others away in charity. Was Sarman the elephant that Durgawati received from Raghunandan Rai? Some local legends do connect the two, though there are no contemporary records to offer conclusive proof. Raghunandan, though, was very clear about what the elephant gift to the Gond queen was all about. In this sloka, for example, he boasts about the generosity of his new patron and snarkily tells Durgawati not to be scared of the horde of elephants he brings with him: '*Srimad Bastar bhumahendra badnangbhoj prasado daya/ dayate Raghunandanay gaj ghanta ghatarava sruyate*' ('On the arrival of Raghunandan Rai with the elephants received in charity from the king of Bastar, oh Queen, do not be afraid. This is the sound of elephant bells, not the roar of thunder up in the sky'). Clearly, Rai never forgave Durgawati for slighting him. Given that he later made a name for himself as part of Akbar's team of Sanskrit scholars, one wonders if the *Akbarnama*'s stinging criticism of Durgawati as a stubborn and arrogant woman who liked to surround herself with sycophants had as much to do with what Fazl may have

heard from people like Raghunandan as with the fact that she
was his master's adversary and, therefore, necessarily needed
to be demonized. Besides, Abul Fazl was just over thirteen
when the Battle of Narai Nala happened, and everything he
wrote, more than a decade later, would have been coloured
by prejudice, personal as well as political.

A short digression here about Raghunandan and his Agra
stint will not be out of place because he was responsible for
poaching for Akbar the brightest jewel in the Garha court—
his guru Mahesh Thakkur. Thakkur's reputation for learning
had reached the Mughal court, and he was summoned by
Akbar to attend a scholarly debate. Thakkur, understandably
unwilling to upset his royal benefactors in Garha, sent
Raghunandan as his representative instead. The latter landed
up in Agra and became part of Akbar's team of Sanskrit
scholars. Among other things, he also became a chess partner
for Akbar and generally impressed the emperor with his
knowledge and wit. In time, this would earn him an entire
kingdom as reward. Akbar separated Tirhoot from Hajipur
within *suba* Bihar and turned it into a separate state, which
became the kingdom of Darbhanga. This was then offered to
Raghunandan Rai, who donated the jagir to his guru as guru
dakshina. Mahesh Thakkur first demurred but then accepted
the gift, and Man Singh was persuaded to change Rai's name
in Akbar's firman to make things official. He then moved
to Darbhanga as its new ruler, leaving Damodar Thakkur
behind in Garha.

There is no dispute over the fact that Akbar gifted
Darbhanga to Mahesh Thakkur. This is recorded in
Darbhanga's Dhanukka inscription, Mithila's medieval land

records as well as later British survey reports. An account of the district of Purnea[12] by Francis Buchanan, for example, clearly references the story of the jagir coming to Thakkur via a favourite disciple. Given that Akbar's Bihar campaign happened more than a decade after the fall of Durgawati, it is reasonable to assume that Mahesh Thakkur moved to Darbhanga well after the Battle of Narai Nala, though he may have visited the Mughal court during Durgawati's lifetime as well. In his celebrated work *Sarva Desh Vritanta Sangraha,* an abridged translation of the *Akbarnama* (Vol. 1) in Sanskrit, Thakkur gives a rough indication of the timing of his Mughal assignment. 'In the 34th year of Akbar Shah calendar,' he writes, 'the famous chronicle called *Vakyat-e-Babri (Baburnama)* was translated in the popular name of Khan Khanan for everyone's understanding by Mirza Khan, son of Bairam Khan.' Given that Abdul Rahim Khan Khanan finished the translation in the late 1580s, Thakkur was referencing a period nearly a quarter of a century after the Battle of Narai Nala.[13]

Mahesh Thakkur was not the only revered name in Dalpati's court, though. With the borders quiet and his lineage secure thanks to the birth of Bir Narayan, the newly-minted Gond king had time to encourage scholarship and creativity in his kingdom and improve the administrative heft of his government. Apart from the Thakkur brothers, Dalpati—and later Durgawati as queen regent—patronized a long line of poets and scholars, turning Garha into a hub of Sanskrit literature. Kavi Ananta Dixit, whose works were later included in the eighteenth-century compilation *Gadhesh Nrpa Varnam Sangraha Slokah*, was one of the literary notables in Dalpati's court.

Mahesh Thakkur, who was known for his knowledge of Nyaya (jurisprudence), astrology, astronomy, philosophy and Vedanta, wrote several books, including the *Tithiva Darpan*, the *Malmas Sarini*, the *Atichar Nirnyay* along with lesser-known works such as *Prayashchittsar*, *Shudhitva Parichedd*, *Daisar* and *Kirtilata*.[14] But his most celebrated work is the *Sarva Desh Vritanta Sangraha* referenced earlier. To this day, Garha has held on to the memory of this learned man—Tirhutia Tal, Thakur Tal and Maheshpur village all bear his name with pride. Like his brother, Damodar Thakkur was also a learned man and writer of some repute. His best-known essays are the *Divyanirnay* and the *Sangramsahityavivekdipika*. Dalpati's court poet was Keshav Lougakshi, who composed his famous works *Nrisinchampu* and *Mimansarthprakash* during his stay in Garha. Like Mahesh Thakkur, Lougakshi was learned in Hindu philosophy, law and religious systems apart from Sanskrit poetry. This focus on learning and creativity—assiduously continued by Durgawati, who sponsored her own set of scholars—earned Dalpati a reputation for both charity and patronage that lived on for at least a century after him. The Ramnagar inscription, dated around 130 years after Dalpati's death, calls him that 'gem of princes' whose 'hand was constantly moist with the water of bounty' and who was 'diligent in the remembrance of Hari' and therefore 'a refuge to those who were brought under his authority, and a guileless guardian of his dependents'.[15]

The wonder years did not last though. Just eight or nine years after their runaway marriage and seven years after he became king, Dalpati Shah died suddenly. The year was 1550. A land grant mentioned in the Fakirchand Akhara inscription shows that grief-stricken queen mother Padmawati donated the village of Vishnupur, 25 miles or 40 km east of present-day Jabalpur, to Raj Purohit Mahesh Thakkur as part of her son's funerary rites. That heartbreaking titbit is a glimpse of how the royal family battled their personal anguish even as the kingdom plunged into uncertainty after the tragedy. Bir Narayan was barely five years old at the time and Durgawati was just over twenty-six. The next fourteen years would test the young queen's mettle in more ways than one.

Dalpati's sudden death meant that Durgawati did not get enough time even to grieve her loss. She needed to think of her son's legacy and the future of her people, and she did that with remarkable composure and discernment. There are stories about some rift between her and her brother-in-law Chandra Shah. In his famous historical fiction title *Rani Durgawati*, litterateur Vrindavan Lal Varma says that the rift was exacerbated by the fact that Durgawati emphatically gave up purdah after her husband died and she began to rule as queen regent. Indeed, the way the queen has been remembered to this day, perennially clad in chain mail and brandishing a naked sword, probably carries at its heart a long-ago memory of the way Durgawati conducted herself as queen regent.

There may have been undercurrents of hostility between Chandra Shah and Durgawati which flared up when his dreams of ruling as his nephew's regent were dashed by the dowager queen. Historian Suresh Mishra says that Chandra Shah 'aspired to the throne' and 'in all probability he did hatch a plan to capture the throne but could not succeed in his mission because of opposition from the people'. Durgawati, wisely as it turns out, roped in senior members of her late husband's durbar to add heft to her claim. Adhar Kayastha or Adhar Kayesth, who was diwan or prime minister under Dalpati, led the faction in court that backed Bir Narayan—and by extension Durgawati—and he was supported by Man Brahmin, another senior official in the administration. The rest of the court backed these powerful voices, and Bir Narayan was crowned king with his mother as regent. The Ramnagar inscription makes no bones about the hand that orchestrated the new power structure: 'This Purandara of the circuit of the earth having demised, Durgavati consecrated on the seat of royalty their son . . . the illustrious Biranarayana.' If the nobles backing Durgawati thought that they would play kingmaker with an infant on the throne of Garha and a young, inexperienced widow as regent, they were sadly mistaken. Durgawati had no intention of allowing anyone to rule in her stead, and she made it very clear almost immediately. While Adhar Kayastha and Man Brahmin were rewarded with important posts—the former retained his prime ministership and the latter too got a senior position in court—the dowager queen retained real power in her own hands.

The palace coup left Chandra Shah without any real support in the Garha court, and he fled, finally seeking refuge in the southern Gond kingdom of Chanda ruled by Karna Shah. Durgawati did not pursue him. and as long as she lived, he did not set foot in Garha. The Gond queen now consolidated her hold on her court, secured her borders and got down to ruling her kingdom with dauntless determination.

The next nearly-decade-and-a-half would belong to her and her alone.

6

The Boy from Agra

'*Baithe Akbar ho gaye pele, laye hai Singorgarh gher*'

(Akbar sat up and then he surrounded the Singorgarh Fort)

—Gond folk song[1]

Around the time Durgawati and Dalpati Shah set all of Gondwana buzzing with their daring elopement and marriage, far away in Fort Amarkot (modern-day Sindh), a dispossessed emperor was desperately waiting for some good news to come his way. Humayun had tasted back-to-back bloody defeat against Sher Shah Suri in the battles of Chausa and Kannauj just two or three years ago. Even as the much-in-love Durgawati and Dalpati were settling down to a happy married life in Singorgarh, Humayun's fifteen-year-old wife Hamida Banu was pregnant with his son and heir. The Gond royal couple had no idea that the child, to be born on 15 October 1542, would change the course of their destiny. His name: Abu'l-Fath Jalal-ud-din Muhammad Akbar. In time, he would come to be known as Akbar the Great.

The young prince had a somewhat precarious childhood in Kandahar and later Kabul under the guardianship of one or the other of his perennially disaffected uncles and their (thankfully) far more genial wives. The frequent ups and downs in Humayun's military fortune did not help matters much either. Often left to the care of guardians like Kamran and Askari Mirza, who had no problems using their brother Humayun's only heir to negotiate terms with him, Akbar's formative years could not have been either secure or even safe. Kamran actually went so far as to use a five-year-old Akbar as a human shield to stop Humayun's persistent cannon fire during a standoff over Kabul in the summer of 1547. Such charming display of affection for one's infant nephew!

With a family as delightfully duplicitous as this, the child Akbar was often subjected to sharp vicissitudes of fortune. In the winter of 1544–45, just as Sher Shah Suri was busy marshalling his troops on the banks of the Yamuna for his central India campaign, little Akbar (then a mere three years old) and his half-sister Bakshi Banu were tramping through biting wind and ankle-deep snow. The children would brave slippery mountain passes and possible ambush to get to Kabul from Kandahar. Despite the treacherous journey, brother and sister would reach Kabul in safety where they would, after some twists and turns, ultimately be reunited with Humayun. Less than five months later, Sher Shah would be dead and Hind would see a new Afghan emperor—Islam Shah Suri.

For the next nearly ten years Akbar stayed in Kabul learning horse riding and swordsmanship when he wasn't getting his toothache remedied by stepmother Haji Begum. The young prince was not particularly studious, playing truant from his studies to spend time flying pigeons, riding horses, playing with dogs or even hanging around the camel stables. This naturally fetched him the occasional elegantly worded rebuke from his father, who was both a learned man and a lover of books. Not that father and son spent too much time together, what with the spectre of rebellion by Humayun's double-crossing half-brothers looming constantly on the horizon.

Meanwhile, Sher Shah was succeeded by his son Islam Shah Suri, whose suspicion-ridden iron rule more or less ignored central India. Only Shujaat Khan, whom Sher Shah had appointed governor of Malwa the year Akbar was born, popped up on Islam Shah Suri's radar. But Khan was smart enough to dodge the bullet with some deft footwork, a trait that he no doubt bequeathed to his son and heir Baz Bahadur as well. When confronted with the prospect of an imminent military clash with Islam Shah Suri, Shujaat Khan refused to fight, saying that he could not raise his sword against the son of his former master. Islam Shah Suri was sufficiently mollified to allow Shujaat Khan to go unmolested, one of the few Afghan nobles from his father's regime to escape the purge.

In Garha, too, this was time for change. The old king Sangram Shah passed away a year after Durgawati got married. Dalpati Shah, then a strapping young man in his mid-twenties, inherited his father's throne and was anointed *Shri Maharajadhiraj Shri Raja* (as per a copperplate inscription from Jabalpur). It was a somewhat grandiose title that was later retained by his brother Chandra Shah and the subsequent rulers of the line. This was despite the fact that after Durgawati, the Raj Gonds of Garha Katanga became vassal kings of the Mughal empire and Garha itself became part of the Malwa suba. It was more or less entirely administered by Mughal officials for nearly three decades. By 1594, or in the final decade of Akbar's long reign, the earlier practice of appointing Mughal jagirdars to Garha was discontinued, and their authority reverted to the later Gond kings, who ruled a much-truncated kingdom for the next two centuries.

Sher Shah Suri's sudden death was a blessing for the kingdoms of this region, allowing them a great deal of elbow room to consolidate their positions in the years that followed. Even before Sher Shah, these kingdoms had a fairly hands-off relationship with the Delhi Sultanate, maintaining distant cordiality and offering little more than the occasional tactical support. Abul Fazl admits as much in the *Akbarnama*. He writes:

> Since the first appearance of Islam when great rulers conquered India, though their reigns were long, the bird of victory of none of them was able to fly to the pinnacles of those strong forts, nor could the hoof of the horse of their thought brush the soil of that extensive country.[2]

In what was fairly unusual for the tumultuous middle ages, Dalpati's short reign of around seven years was largely uneventful. He spent the time refurbishing his capital fort of Singorgarh, inviting Sanskrit scholars to his court, giving grants and paying his respects to an assortment of holy men. Even though he died a good half a decade before Humayun—

and a year later Akbar—came to power, folklore has spun an interesting connect between him and the Mughal court. According to local legend, Birbal, who later gained fame in Akbar's court as a senior courtier and chief wit, first worked for Dalpati Shah in Singorgarh. The Gond king's able Diwan Adhar Kayastha appointed him officer in charge of religious events. But Birbal soon lost his billet when he, too generously for his own good as it turns out, donated alms worth Rs 25,000 on a particular occasion. (As mentioned earlier medieval coinage comprised silver coins called rupee/rupaiya, gold coins called mohur and copper coins called dam.)

This pocket pinch annoyed Dalpati Shah so much that he fired Birbal immediately. Birbal then went to Delhi and later found favour with Akbar.[3] There is some disagreement over this incident because Birbal was originally from Rewa, not Garha. But even if it is half-imagined, it still spins a serendipitous connect between Akbar's Agra and the Raj Gonds of Garha.

Birbal was of course not the only connect, spiritual and intellectual, that the Gond court shared with Akbar, but more about that later. Also, while Akbar is universally acknowledged as tolerant and liberal—qualities rare in the medieval world—the truth is there were many lesser-known monarchs in India who espoused similar views, Dalpati and later Durgawati included. It was religious tolerance born out of political expediency, administrative requirements and a genuine love of scholarship. Dalpati, for example, made donations to Sri Baba Kapur Sahib who, says historian Suresh Mishra, was most certainly either a Sufi saint or a Kabirpanthi. A copper grant discovered in Jabalpur more than sixty years ago mentions that 'Maharaja Dalapatasadeva' gifted the two villages of Kuda and Kachanari to the holy man backed by a diktat that every household in these villages would donate a half-price coin to him.[4]

Dalpati, however, died suddenly not long after this grant. According to local records, he passed away on a full moon night in the month of Paush or January, Samvat 1605, or in the year 1550.[5] This personal tragedy plunged Durgawati into public life, giving her a taste of the kind of intrigue and treachery it would bring in its wake.

When Akbar took over the reins, Durgawati had already been running her kingdom for nearly six years as her son's regent. Akbar came to power suddenly and in the middle of considerable political upheaval. Humayun, who had wrested back control of the empire after Islam Shah Suri died, himself passed away a year later, leaving the throne to his teenage son. Akbar's initial years as the emperor saw enough turmoil for him to be both battle-hungry and wary of losing his legacy the way his father had. By the time Akbar gave his nod to the Garha campaign, he had seen his closest advisors in court turn into power-hungry back-stabbing predators. Immediately after the emperor turned eighteen, Bairam Khan, Humayun's trusted general and Akbar's guardian and regent all through his rule as a minor, had rebelled. Though pardoned, he later met a grisly end in January 1561. The very next year, the young emperor killed his milk brother Adham Khan, his wet nurse Maham Anaga's son. Within months of taking control of his legacy, Akbar had tasted treachery in his own backyard.

Contrary to the Bollywood template of the great Mughal being a bellowing but benign pater familias firmly in control of both his family and his realm, the young Akbar who was consolidating his empire in the mid-sixteenth century was actually a very different man. For one, he had a very clear idea of whom he saw as a threat. For another, he genuinely believed that as a medieval monarch, he needed to earn his spurs through conquest. 'A monarch should be ever intent on conquest otherwise his neighbours rise in arms against him,' Abul Fazl quotes him saying. And then, 'The army should be exercised in warfare lest from want of training they become self-indulgent.'[6] And finally, by his own admission, this early Akbar was very far from being the tolerant monarch he later became. His various proclamations from this time display the uncertainties and insecurities of a young ruler trying to find his feet among the shifting sands of medieval politics. Later on, he would look back on this younger self with contrition. Abul Fazl quotes him in the *Ain-i-Akbari* saying, 'Formerly I persecuted men into conformity with my faith and deemed it Islam. As I grew in knowledge, I was overwhelmed with shame.'[7]

From the early 1560s right up to the late-1570s, Akbar was busy doing a balancing act between largely placating orthodox Sunni sentiments in his court—particularly the likes of Shaikh Abdu'n Nabi, whose hold on the young emperor increased after the exit of Bairam Khan—with the occasional pro-Hindu announcement, such as the abolition of the jizya tax or the issue of a land grant farman for the Madan Mohan temple at Vrindavan. It is interesting that Akbar waged war against Durgawati the same year that he abolished jizya for the first time and seven months later followed it up by signing off 200 bighas of tax-free land for the Madan Mohan temple, a clear carrot-and-stick policy if ever there was one. Three years later, he unleashed the full fury of his military might on crushing the Sisodias, describing the fall of Chittor as a victory of Islam over infidels. The Fathnama-i-Chitor issued on 9 March 1568, just a month after the fall of Chittor, gives enough indication of this hardline spin in Akbar's own words:

> We spend our precious time to the best of our ability in war (*ghaza*) and jihad and with the help of eternal god, who is the supporter of our ever increasing empire, we are busy in subjugating the localities, habitations, forts and towns which are under the possession of the infidels, may god forsake and annihilate all of them, and thus raising the standard of Islam everywhere and removing the darkness of polytheism and violent sins by the use of the sword. We destroy the places of worship of idols in those places and other parts of India.

Rana Udai Singh's refusal to 'kiss the royal threshold', says this victory message, giving a religious twist to the politics of power, 'increased his [Akbar's] zeal for the divine religion'.[8]

Interestingly, the carrots offered to the Hindus dried up after Chittor, as many Rajput clans fell in line. There are examples of Rajput royals like Mota Raja Udai Singh Rathore of Marwar or Kalyan Mal of Bikaner joining the imperial service. For Akbar, that meant less need to appease the Rajputs and a greater need to placate Indian Muslims instead. This explains, in part, the rise and rise of Shaikh Abdu'n Nabi. In 1574, the emperor directed Nabi (who, by then, was the *sadr* or chief religious officer in court) to reimpose the jizya. And yet, when the sadr was summarily dismissed from service in December 1579, Akbar followed it up with abolishing the jizya once again in 1580.

Of course, as Rajputs began to get integrated into the mainstream of imperial politics, their sway on Akbar's court also got stronger. What tempered the control of hardliners like Shaikh Abdu'n Nabi on state policy was the increasing influence of Rajput wives and senior Hindu courtiers on a more confident and less insecure Akbar. But as we have seen, even this temperance would often see a flip-flop. There are many examples of the emperor giving in to suggestions from hardliners not only regarding Hindus but also Shias and Mahadavis. Just before embarking on his Gujarat campaign, for example, he proclaimed that the battle was necessary not merely to crush the remaining detritus of Afghan nobility in that region but to avenge orthodox Sunnis living there who were being tormented by Afghan converts to Mahdavism. And in the early 1570s, he issued a farman to Qazi Abdul Sanad, the *muhtasib* of Bilgram, to 'prevent the Hindus of that pargana from practicing idol worship and take such other steps as might help in eradicating the manifestations of heresy and deviation from that pargana'.[9] For the early Akbar, political and religious exigencies often fitted neatly into a common goal. It is only when an older and far more mature emperor began his Sulh-i-kul (harmonious existence of all faiths) journey did he move away from the need to feed Sunni orthodoxy. Unfortunately for Durgawati, it was not this man whose armies she encountered in Narai Nala but his earlier, more insecure and intolerant avatar.

Interestingly, folk lore in central India has spun an origin story for Akbar that can rival Abul Fazl's salacious gossip about Dalpati Shah's antecedents. Alexander Cunningham records this in his *Report of a Tour in the Central Provinces and Lower Gangetic Doab 1881–82*. The people of Asni, he writes, believe that when Sher Shah defeated Humayun and the Mughal fled, he left behind a 'begam named Choli in Delhi who was captured by the conqueror'. Later Sher Shah gifted her away to his bard Narhari who carried her to 'Bandhugarh in Rewa' where she gave birth to Akbar. The dispossessed prince grew up in Rewa and 12 years later sought Baghel Raja Vir Bhanu/Birbhan's help to recover the throne of Delhi. This was granted and Akbar reunited with Humayun to defeat Islam Shah. The story establishes the fact that there was some understanding between the Baghels and Humayun which is documented in other contemporary accounts as well.[10] For the first several years of his rule, Akbar's attention was focused on neutralizing two threats—the remnants of the Afghan Suri dynasty and rebellions among his own generals. His attacks on the hill chieftains of Punjab or his Rajputana strategy were all partly driven by this twin focus. Even the Sisodias—whom he brutally confronted twice, at Chittor and later at Haldighati—were, in some ways, part of this overarching battle plan. One of the reasons why Akbar relentlessly pursued Rana Udai Singh was also because the latter had given shelter to Baz Bahadur of Malwa, Shujaat Khan's son and heir. Given the Malwa royal family's close connect with Sher Shah, who had appointed Shujaat Khan governor in the first place, and their ability to survive Islam Shah's later purge, Baz Bahadur was as much on Akbar's hit list as Rana Udai Singh and later his son and heir Rana Pratap. The Mughal emperor would have been uneasy about Baz Bahadur, suspecting him of playing both ends against the middle, as indeed he did.

But Durgawati does not fit this template at all. So why did Akbar attack her? She did not ally with the dregs of the earlier Afghan ruling elite. In fact, she actually locked horns with the Miyana Afghans and gave them a thrashing when they got ideas about her being easy prey as a woman and a widow. Nor did she give refuge to someone Akbar was looking to crush. Just a few years before Asaf Khan attacked her, Durgawati had actually given Baz Bahadur a bloody nose on the battlefield. He lost so decisively that contemporary historians say he proceeded to drown himself in wine and song to forget the humiliation—very filmy of him indeed. Given that in a few years he would reinvent himself in Akbar's court and find fresh fame for a new style of music called Baazkhani, this 'spin-doctoring' seems entirely in character. Lover of Rupmati, musician of near-Tansen calibre, sharp-nosed politician, Baz Bahadur was clearly a man of many parts.

Her brush with Baz Bahadur aside, Durgawati deftly ensured that she stayed politically neutral in the skirmishes between the old Afghan nobility and the new Mughal one. Besides, all the officials Akbar sent to the Gond court spoke highly of the queen as an administrator. She was, by all accounts, happy when the Mughal emperor accepted her son Bir Narayan's claim to the throne as Dalpati Shah's heir. According to Gond folklore, two scholars from Akbar's court named Gop Mahapatra and Narhari Mahapatra visited Durgawati. Narhari was the first, and since he visited immediately after Akbar recognized her young son's claim to the throne of Garha, he received a lavish welcome from Durgawati. The story goes that the queen presented the scholar with gifts worth a crore of rupees—quite literally a king's or queen's ransom. Gop Mahapatra came later, and his mission was a little more delicate: to find out just how well Durgawati was ruling her kingdom. Once again, both the queen and her able diwan, Adhar Kayastha, rolled out the proverbial red carpet. Gop Mahapatra went back with a very favourable impression indeed.

Gop Mahapatra sang Adhar Kayastha's praises so long and so often, goes the folk tradition, that Akbar became curious about this paragon of ministerial virtue and sent Durgawati a couplet requesting that he visit Agra. '*Apni seema raj ki amal karo farman/Bhejo nag supet soyi, aru Adhar diwan*' ('Stay within the bounderies of your kingdom and send your diwan Adhar to me') went the couplet telling the queen just what to do.[11] Of course, Adhar Kayastha was then dispatched to Agra, where he dazzled everyone with his wit. The story narrates how Akbar decided to test Adhar Kayastha by sitting incognito among his nobles and leaving the throne empty. When the diwan walked in, he was at first taken aback but quickly recovered his wits and saluted the emperor. A surprised Akbar is supposed to have asked him how he knew who to salute. 'It's simple—even though you were sitting among your nobles, every eye in the durbar kept turning towards you so it was not difficult to guess who you were,' replied Kayastha. Akbar, or so the legend goes, was so impressed with this answer that he conferred a robe of honour on the Garha diwan.

There's a sequel to this story, where Akbar is shown quizzing Adhar Kayastha about the Garha queen and her kingdom. Kayastha, showing a remarkably sharp mind that would have made Birbal proud, offered the emperor a golden ripe bitter gourd. The not-so-subtle hint: that Garha's terrain was as rugged as the skin of the gourd and the kingdom was as rich as its golden hue, but bite into it and you get a taste of just how bitter its defence can be. The embellishments aside, what the story does establish is that there was certainly some relationship between the kingdom of Garha and the Mughal court long before Asaf Khan's invasion and Durgawati's final sacrifice. It also hints at just how interested and curious Akbar may have been about this faraway kingdom and the remarkable lady who ruled it.

This cultural give and take actually makes the invasion that followed a little more difficult to understand. What did this ruler of a remote kingdom do that made it imperative for Akbar to crush her? After all, Garha was not geographically strategic for Akbar. Did Durgawati's neighbours gang up against her and add to what Mughal general Asaf Khan, for his own interests, as it turns out, was feeding the young emperor?

Asaf Khan's advice aside, Akbar's Garha strategy fits into a pattern he followed with other conquests as well: sending Mughal generals as jagirdars or administrators to the region closest to the target and then following it up with a military campaign. Just three years after the Battle of Narai Nala, Akbar kicked off his Chittor campaign with the appointment of Asaf Khan Harvi as jagirdar of Bayana in the autumn of 1567. Bayana was the Mughal jagir closest to Chittor. Similarly in 1585, Mirza Aziz Koka was given the sarkar of

Garha and Raisin of Malwa as his jagir to allow him to launch his Deccan offensive. And just two years after the siege of Chittorgarh, Akbar offered Mughal generals Majnun Khan Qaqshal, Shaham Khan Jalair and other officers jagirs near the Kalinjar Fort before ordering them to wrest the fort from Raja Ram Chand. The indications are clear: Whatever Asaf Khan's role in convincing Akbar about a Garha campaign, the young emperor may not have needed much convincing to begin with. Asaf Khan's posting as the jagirdar of Sarkar Karra may have come parcelled with a military mission to bring central India under Mughal control. That's why it was predictably followed by first the conquest of Panna and then Garha.

Durgawati's own role in this military manoeuvre is no less significant. In his translation of the Ramnagar inscription, Fitz Edward Hall says that Durgawati was singled out for chastisement because she had the temerity to take on her neighbours. 'As queen regnant, her husband having demised, she ventured on a foray against Bhelsa. In reprisal for this incursion, Asaf Khan was sent, by the Emperor Akbar, to chastise her hardihood,' writes Hall.[12] Cunningham, for his part, calls Asaf Khan a 'rapacious chief' and the invasion an 'unhallowed expedition without even the shadow of a pretext' except that the 'country was said to be rich and it was presumably defenceless as its ruler was a woman'.[13]

Other historians say her neighbours may have been rattled by her ability to fend off both the Miyana Afghans and more importantly Baz Bahadur. Then as now, a successful woman is often seen as a threat by the men around her. According to Suresh Mishra, Durgawati's victory over Baz Bahadur, ironically, was at the root of her problems with Akbar. As a widow and queen regnant, her ability to humiliate a powerful neighbour like Baz Bahadur would have made her quite the talk of the town, causing the young Mughal emperor, still far from secure in his skin, to turn his attention towards central India in general and Garha in particular.

The rani's growing military clout would have also made her immediate neighbours uneasy, particularly the ruler of Ratanpur, Haihai Raja Kalyan Sahai, son of Bahar Sahai, who actually visited the Mughal court in 1563. Garha's relations with this neighbour were by no means cordial, so this was a crucial diplomatic visit. It was intended not only to offer obeisance to Akbar but also get his assurance that Ratanpur would get Mughal protection in case of any aggression by Garha.[14]

Did the rani's growing reputation in the battlefield annoy Akbar, who was only a few years older than her son? Was it just expansionist battle thirst that led the Mughal emperor to order the destruction of Durgawati, or was it also because she was a woman in charge of a prosperous realm? Even if he was swayed by Asaf Khan's descriptions of Garha's wealth—and may not have wished to go against one of his seasoned senior generals—this was a decision Akbar would have trouble living up to, given Khan's subsequent perfidy. Historian Vincent Smith is deservedly scathing about this unnecessary show of machismo. 'Akbar's attack on a princess of a character so noble was mere aggression, wholly unprovoked and devoid of all justification other than the lust for conquest and plunder,' he writes in *Akbar The Great Mogul*.[15] 'Akbar shared the opinion of all Asiatic and not a few European monarchs that it is the duty of a king to extend his dominions.' Local Gond folklore offers an interesting perspective on what provoked the attack on Rani Durgawati. According to the story, Akbar gifted Rani Durgawati a golden spinning wheel by way of an oblique message that, as a woman, her job was to restrict herself to household chores like spinning cotton. Running a kingdom, underlined the message, was not a woman's job. She, on the other hand, sent him a return gift of a golden cotton carding tool implying that, as a Muslim, his job was to card cotton rather than occupy a throne. Since there is no contemporary evidence that confirms this story, it is probably apocryphal. What it does, though is give us a picture of the kind of queen her people took Durgawati to be—someone unapologetic about her role as the de facto ruler of Garha, confident as an able administrator and strong enough to eyeball her opponent even if he happened to be the Mughal emperor. Indeed, Gond folk songs specifically mention this, snarkily telling Akbar that he should take a lesson in administration from Durgawati. '*Tum ka raj karat ho Akbar, durgan patiya churaye*' (What do you know about ruling O Akbar, learn a thing or two from Durgawati'), says a popular ballad. To this day Gonds believe Akbar attacked Garha because he coveted Sarman, Durgawati's precious war elephant.

Durgawati's reputation not only as an able administrator but as a woman who did not take kindly to neighbourly bullying would not have endeared her to the men around her, including the young Mughal emperor. As we shall see, being a strong woman ultimately sealed this queen's fate.

7

Reign of the Rani

'*Vigya Durgawati ragyi Garha rajye trayogunah*'

(The learned Durgawati reigns in the kingdom of Garha,
a land of amazing accomplishments)

—*Gadhesh Nrpa Varnan Sangraha Slokah*

The year 1550 began in the worst possible way for Rani
Durgawati. For the twenty-six-year-old grieving widow,
life would have looked like an insurmountable hurdle at
this point. Durgawati was still very young and had had no
experience of governing the kingdom. Indeed she had had
very little political exposure when her father-in-law and then
husband were on the throne. But now she knew she needed
to act swiftly and decisively. Garha was surrounded by
neighbours who were envious of its prosperity. Till Dalpati's
demise, these hawks had been kept in check by the kingdom's
military reputation, mostly forged during Sangram Shah's
rule. Durgawati knew these neighbours were now watching
the power play in Singorgarh with hawk-eyed interest.

Durgawati's rule began in right earnest the day her trusted official Man Brahman anointed Bir Narayan, her five-year-old son, the new raja of Garha/Gadha Katanga. Contemporary sources do not give us a description of the coronation, but going by the guidelines laid out in the *Prastab Ratnakar*, the ceremony would have been held on a Sunday, Wednesday, Thursday or Friday under the planetary influence or Vedic nakshatra of Rohini, Pushya, Anuradha and Dhanishtha. According to the Fakirchand Akhara inscription, Dalpati Shah died on a full moon night in the month of *Paush* or January, Samvat 1605 (year 1550). Since the auspicious months for coronation, according to the *Prastab Ratnakar*, are *Paush* (January–February), *Jayestha* (May–June), *Shravan* (July–August) or *Ashwin* (September–October), it is not unreasonable to assume that by mid-October 1550, the boy-king was already on the throne of Garha. And Gond Rani Durgawati was firmly in charge of the realm as regent.

Contemporary descriptions paint an Arcadian portrait of Durgawati's kingdom at the heart of India. Poet Keshav Dixit, for instance, offers this lyrical description of the queen and her kingdom in the *Gadhesh Nrpa Varnan Sangraha Slokah*: '*Urbara sarvato bhumih madhyato Narmada nadi/ Vigya Durgawati ragyi Garha rajye trayogunah*' ('The kingdom of Garha has fertile farm lands everywhere with the Narmada river flowing through it and it is ruled by the learned queen Durgawati whose realm is full of accomplishments').

Abul Fazl gives a more detailed account of the kingdom of Garha. 'The east part of the country adjoins Ratanpur which belongs to Jharkhand, and the west is contiguous to Raisen which belongs to the province of Malwa,' he writes in the *Akbarnama*.[1] 'Its length may be 150 kos (480 km east west). On the north is the country of Panna and on the south the Deccan. Its width may be 80 kos' (256 km north south). The country, he says, is called Gadha Katanga. 'It is an extensive tract and is full of forts and contains populous cities and towns.' According to the *Akbarnama*, Garha contained 70,000 inhabited villages. The kingdom acquired its medieval name from the city of Gadha and the village of Katanga.

Durgawati, as we saw in the earlier chapters, was backed by some of the ablest and senior-most ministers in her court—a support that allowed her to clash with her brother-in-law Chandra Shah, rebuff his claim to the throne and force him into exile in Chanda, a Gond kingdom to the south of Garha ruled by Karn/Karna Shah. The *Gadhesh Nrpa Varnam* mentions this support, saying that Bir Narayan's rule was 'guided by his mother and the best of his ministers of exceptional intelligence (*jananya subuddhina mantrireno saddhyam*)'.

The presence of Chandra Shah so close to her borders must have made Durgawati uneasy, and this was possibly one of the reasons why she sought recognition of Bir Narayan's claim from the Mughal emperor who sent Gop Mahapatra and Narhari Mahapatra as imperial officials to her court. There is no doubt that an official named Narhari Mahapatra was part of Akbar's court. Akbar apparently banned cow slaughter after reading one of Narhari's poems.[2]

This early interest in her realm and rule by the distant Mughal monarch should have sent a warning signal to Durgawati. After all, the kingdom that she inherited on her son's behalf was considerable, covering 43 garh or fortress districts, each comprising 350–700 villages. These fortress districts were administrative units controlled either directly by the queen or through subordinate feudal lords (jagirdars) and junior rajas. The Gond administrative structure was considerably more federal than non-tribal kingdoms. Durgawati, for instance, had 23,000 cultivated villages in her possession, of which 11,000 were directly under her control. The remaining 12,000 were administered by local sardars, who often called themselves 'raja' or 'rai' and who owed alliance to the throne of Garha. The raja of Lanji mentioned in earlier chapters was one such junior raja under Dalpati and later Durgawati's rule. These subordinate rajas were in charge of general law and order in the land under their control and governed through village headmen or *gram mukhiyas*. The *gram mukhiya* was also called 'patel', and this official was responsible for tax collection in what was mostly a hereditary role. The common cultivator shared a part of his produce with either the jagirdar or directly with the queen. Apart from being the village taxman, the patel also doubled as policeman and judge for local disputes and received a regular salary or a parcel of land as compensation.[3] The sardars or subordinate Rajas also contributed arms and men to the king or queen of Garha in times of war. The recruitment, training and arming of these men was largely done by the sardar, and it was the feudal lords of the Garh that also paid their salaries. This decentralized structure was actually a huge disadvantage. It meant that Durgawati's troops were not of uniform quality in terms of training and battle-readiness, a factor that became critical in the final battle of Narai Nala as we shall see. It also meant that the feudal lords retained an unusual amount of hold over individual sections of the royal army, another factor that affected the outcome of the final battle.

Garha's loose federal structure was a throwback to the time when the entire Gondwana region was a fractured polity ruled by minor rajas. Abul Fazl says as much in the *Akbarnama*:

> 'There was not in former times any sole ruler, on the contrary there were many Rajahs and Rais. At the present day, when by the revolutions of time the country is no longer under the old regime [a reference to the Mughal takeover of Gondwana] there are still many Rajahs. For example the Raja of Gadha, the Raja of Garola, the Raja of Harya, the Raja of Salwani, the Raja of Danaki, the Raja of Khatola, the Raja of Mugda, the Raja of Mandla, the Raja of Deohar, the Raja of Lanjhi.

This fractured feudal set-up continued right through the Maratha era. A mid-1800s list shows there were as many as twenty-five local rajas in the area currently covered by Jabalpur, Mandla, Seoni, Hoshangabad, Sagar, Damoh and Narsinghpur. Feudal tax for later Raj Gond rulers by then was down to some ghee and a few bamboo sticks.

According to the *Ain-i-Akbari* (Volume 2), under Mughal rule, the sarkar of Garha contained fifty-seven mahals, with a revenue of 10,077,080 dams with a cavalry of 5,495 and infantry of 2,54,500. Each of the mahals contributed cavalry and infantry as well as tax revenue, which gives us a good idea of how the whole tax-and-soldiers system worked in medieval

Gondwana. This system of ruling through subordinate kings was fairly entrenched under the Raj Gonds and was doubtless the structure that Durgawati both inherited and left behind. According to Abul Fazl, people paid their taxes in either gold mohurs or forest and agricultural produce, including elephants. Under later Gond rulers, when the kingdom began to shrink and its prosperity dwindled, the jagirdars simply offered soldiers and not much else to the throne of Garha. Sleeman describes the arrangement thus: 'Under these Gond Rajas the country seems for the most part to have been distributed among feudatory chiefs bound to attend upon the prince at his capital with a stipulated number of troops to be employed whenever their services might be required.'[4]

Durgawati's tax regime was not draconian, and folk traditions mention instances of the queen waiving off taxes during drought or famine. Even fodder for the royal animals—military and milch—was paid for by the treasury and not extracted as an additional tax, which was the norm in many neighbouring kingdoms. Contrast this with the picture painted by folk songs from the late nineteenth and early twentieth centuries, and you begin to understand why the Gonds remember the glory rule of their favourite rani with such fervour. In *Folk Songs of the Maikal Hills*, Shamrao Hivale and Verrier Elwin documented one such song: 'In this kingdom of the English, how hard it is to live/To pay cattle tax we have to sell a cow/To pay forest tax we have to sell a bullock/To pay land tax we have to sell a buffalo/How are we to get our food?'[5] In contrast, the Raj Gond rule was an 'easy eventless sway', as Sleeman describes it. As a result, the 'rich

Durgawati Murti in Samadhi Sthal, Jabalpur

Samadhi Shtal of Bir Narayan in Jabalpur

TOMB OF QUEEN DURGAVATI

B/W photo of Samadhi Sthal circa 1916

Recent photo of Madan Mahal

B/W photo of Madan Mahal circa 1865

Chogan Ka Kila

Singorgarh Fort

Sharada Mata Mandir with red pennants

Bhawartal Garden

Durgawati Murti in Bhawartal Garden

A temple in Chhattisgarh where Durgawati is worshipped

Statue of Rani Durgawati at the Rani Durgavati
Vishwavidyalaya, Jabalpur

country over which they ruled prospered, its flocks and herds increased and the treasury filled'.

Part of those riches came from agriculture, which flourished during Durgawati's reign thanks to her focus on digging tanks and lakes and carrying out restoration work on many of the existing step wells and water bodies in Gondwana. As a result, there were a total sixty-four lakes and tanks dotting the craggy landscape of Garha when she was in charge, ensuring enough water for irrigation even in that perennially parched land. The Raj Gonds used a simple expedient to increase the area under cultivation and keep their farmlands well-watered. The local populace was encouraged to clear virgin forests for cultivation and clean up water bodies for irrigation. The carrot was that the land cleared and so watered would belong to whoever took the trouble to make it arable.

As a result, Garha came to be known not only for food grains like wheat and rice, which it would export to Gujarat and the Deccan, but also many types of fruits and vegetables and cash crops like sugarcane and cotton. Garha's jaggery or gur was famed, as was its dairy produce such as ghee and curd. An old local ditty gives a good idea of what the Gond produced for sale: '*Chaitay gur, baisakhakhe tel/Jaithey lata Asare bel/Sawan saag aur Bhadon mahi/Kunwar karela Kartik dahi*' ('Jaggery in March, cooking oil in April, leafy greens in May and wood apples in June, then the rain clouds come and it's time for spinach, August brings bitter gourds and September–October is the time for curd').[6] As for cotton, textile weaving was a hereditary occupation of the Koshta community, and to this day these clusters in and around Garha produce colourful hand-woven cotton saris.

Apart from agricultural export, the region was also famed for its forest produce and, of course, elephants. In fact, the royal emblem of the Raj Gonds of Garha was a one-horned tiger clawing an elephant, a clear nod to the kingdom's woodland wealth. Abul Fazl says the forests—stretching from Narwar to Berar and in Handia, Uchchod, Chanderi, Satwas, Bijagarh, Raisen, Hoshangabad, Garha and Hariagarh—in the Malwa suba had a large elephant population. Given how critical elephants were to medieval warfare, much of Garha's riches must have come from elephant trade. As earlier mentioned, a cache of gold and silver coins discovered over a hundred years ago near Madan Mahal gave historians a good idea of Garha's trade treasure. The buried hoard, discovered in 1908, bore the names of the 'Sultans of Delhi, Gujarat and Kashmir and the Bahmanis of Kulbarga, the Khiljis of Malwa and the Sharqis of Jaunpur, ranging in date from 1311 to 1553', and 'three of the gold coins are suspected to be Nepalese', reported the *District Gazetteer of Jubbulpore*. The loot that Asaf Khan amassed after the sacking of Chauragarh also gives an idea of Garha's wealth. According to Abul Fazl, that hoard included coined and un-coined gold, decorated utensils, jewels, pearl figures, pictures, jewelled and decorated statues, figures of animals made wholly of gold and 100 jars full of Allauddin's ashrafis, apart from the 1,000 elephants that both turned Asaf Khan's head and caused him untold grief, as we shall see later.

Garha was among the few Hindu kingdoms that was rich enough to mint its own coins in gold and silver with legends in Devanagari or Telegu imprinted on them. The Ramnagar inscription, a near-contemporary source which gives a fairly detailed picture of the rani, her realm and its riches, also mentions both the gold coins and the elephants that Garha was famed for:

> Durgavati, by her own renown was famed in the three worlds; she made this whole earth change its appearance by immensely high golden dwellings as an unlimited splendid Hemachala, by the heaps of gems scattered everywhere and by the herds of frolicsome elephants just like the herds of elephants possessed by Indra.[7]

Present-day Gond balladeers like Manoj Maravi also talk about the queen's peaceful and prosperous rule. In his song *Mandla ke Rani Durgawati*, he says her rule was so good that people were happy and all sections of society were taken care of (*'dukhi nahin koi unka raj ma unnat sakal samaj'*). That sounds pretty similar to how Cunningham describes the veerangana's rule[8]—'She governed the country with singular skill and prudence.' In a sense, bard songs and references to Rani Durgawati's reign have remained unchanged in theme and tenor for the past four-and-a-half centuries—a good indication of how her people have remembered her through time.

Apart from the lakes that she constructed, Durgawati is also credited with building several temples in Mandla, Narsinghpur and Garha. According to local lore, the Sharada Mata Mandir near Madan Mahal in Jabalpur was built by her after the goddess who was her *kuldevi* or family deity commanded the queen to do so. The Shiv temple on the banks of the Narmada on the southern side of Barman

Ghat in Narsinghpur district is another example. Called
Rani Durgawati Temple by local devotees, it was originally
built by her, though the current structure is far more recent.
Local historians say the queen also restored a number of
smaller temples and maths all over the kingdom, which is
entirely possible given that she is believed, in local lore, to
have frequented several well-known temples in the region,
including the Bajnamath Temple in Tilwara Ghat and the
Chausath Yogini Temple in Bhedaghat. Apart from temples
and maths, the queen also carried out extensive secular
construction, including refurbishments of the Chauragarh
Fort and Madan Mahal where she lived. Local historians say
the queen preferred to spend the scorching summer months
in Madan Mahal because of its height and greenery and would
often go on private boat rides on the nearby Sangram Sagar
Lake, particularly on full moon nights. Given the persistent
rumours about the queen using underground tunnels to visit
temples and ghats, it's quite possible that much of this local
lore is rooted in regular public sightings of the rani, another
indication that she turned away from strict purdah in her role
as regent.

Durgawati, though, was fortunate, because for the first
ten years of her rule, Delhi was too busy minding its own
business to look too closely at outlier kingdoms like Gadha.
When Akbar became emperor, he was a mere boy. When he
took back control of his empire, his focus was on tackling
the rivalry and treachery of his top nobles rather than on
any expansionist plans. As a result, Durgawati got enough
elbow room to strengthen her grip on her kingdom both in
terms of governance as well as militarily, as we shall see. The

queen, wisely as it turns out, took several steps to stabilize the
political situation and secure her borders.

First, she recruited some able generals, including several
Muslim Miyana Afghan commanders who remained loyal to
her till the end. Among her generals who find mention in
folklore or contemporary sources are Afghan commanders
like Shams Khan Miyana and Mubarak Khan, both of whom
died in the Battle of Narai Nala. Then there were Senapati
Chakraman and Miyana Afghan general Bukhari Rumi,
both of whom were honoured with tanks named after them.
Rumi, along with another veteran general Bhoj Kayesth, was
in charge of the Chauragarh Fort which, during Durgawati's
time, was the capital of the kingdom. The queen dispatched
Bir Narayan to their care when the boy-king was wounded
in the battle of Narai. Bir Narayan, for his part, entrusted
them with the job of conducting a jauhar in the fort before
he charged out to meet his destiny in the final faceoff against
Asaf Khan.[9]

Others who fought in the battle with Asaf Khan included
Kanur Kalyan Bakhila, Khan Jahan Dakit and Maharakha
Brahman—an indication that the rani was not without her
team of brave and loyal followers. Arjundas Bais, who was the
fauzdar or military commander, was in charge of the queen's
famed elephant corps. A brave soldier, he died defending the
Singorgarh Fort. His counterpart Shams Khan Miyana was in
charge of the royal cavalry and, as mentioned earlier, died in
the battle of Narai.

Given how many of these names are remembered through
local references and collective memory, it's clear Durgawati
substantially increased the number of generals and officials

in her command in an effort to strengthen the security of her kingdom. The recruitment of Afghan commanders and soldiers into her army after she bested them in battle shows that the queen was both tolerant and practical. Like her husband, she did not allow religious considerations to come in the way of both appointments and promotions in her court. In this, she was no different from her adversary Emperor Akbar, although while his liberal world view has acquired him acclaim as a most unusual medieval monarch, hers remains largely unknown outside Gondwana. Durgawati's example shows that religious tolerance was by no means unheard of in medieval India, and many smaller kingdoms practised this both in their charitable contributions as well as in recruitment into military and civilian ranks.

Apart from the generals mentioned above, Durgawati's court had several senior officials as well. As mentioned earlier, Mahesh Thakkur, was the *raj purohit* or royal priest, and Adhar Kayastha, was the diwan or prime minister, These were the two most important civilian officials in the realm. The raj purohit was not only in charge of all religious and sacred rites and rituals in the kingdom (including temple consecration, weddings and funeral rites and fire sacrifices) but also acted as the monarch's personal advisor on secular matters as well. The diwan, on the other hand, handled all administrative and taxation-related matters as well as the day-to-day running of the kingdom. The queen trusted him implicitly and allowed him to handle general governance in her name.

Local historians say that, going by later Raj Gond legal structure, it is clear that Durgawati's rule had a precedent-led judicial system. Local bard songs talk about the queen hearing public complaints herself and offering her judgment with the support of her diwan and raj purohit. While local village issues would typically be resolved by the village patel, disputes regarding taxes or official corruption were handled by the diwan. Capital punishment was not common—in fact exile was the harshest judgment normally decreed. Fines and verbal warnings were the most common punishments.

There are references to other important posts in the court of Garha/Gadha, though the monarchs mentioned are later Gond kings. For instance, there are references to the *jyotihshi* or court astrologer and multiple purohits who probably reported to the raj purohit during the reign of Hirday Shah; Pradhan or feudal lord, during the rule of Narendrashah; *bhandaragarik* or keeper of the royal warehouse and *karmakandi* or performer of rituals, also during Hirday Shah's rule; and *dharmashastri* or religious jurist when Nizamshah was in power. While the references connect these posts to kings who ruled a century or more after Durgawati, there is no reason to assume that the administrative structure would have changed completely in the interim.[10]

Besides beefing up the army, Durgawati also shifted her capital from Singorgarh to Chauragarh. This was primarily to improve location advantage: If Singorgarh was protected by forest cover, Chauragarh was protected by terrain. Perched atop a craggy peak of the Satpura range in present-day Narsinghpur disctrict, Chauragarh lay near the western edge of the kingdom and was truly impregnable in terms of access. Even today, the steep climb and jagged approach makes any outing to Chauragarh a hair-raising affair. Even so, she faced several military skirmishes during her nearly decade-and-a-half reign. She managed to rebuff all of them, except the last one, thanks as much to her leadership as to her ability to pick loyal and efficient generals to lead her forces, as we shall see in the next chapter. The Ramnagar inscription gives a vivid description of how she would ride out atop her favourite elephant to lead her soldiers in battle.

That image of the queen offering both protection and prosperity lives on to this day. Take Acharya Bhagwat Dubey, a present-day renowned poet in the region, whose songs are popular among both Gond and non-Gond listeners. In his celebratory song about Durgawati, he highlights this twin appeal of the rani, suggesting that her popularity made Akbar jealous. After the rani came to Garha, goes the poem, '*Gond raj mein cha gayo naw umang utsah*' ('the Gond kingdom was filled with new hope and aspiration'), prompting the Mughal durbar to take note. '*Akbar ke khatkan lago jo Garh Mandal khush haal/Kaan bhar kay Akbar ke Asaf Khan chal paro/ Nagare pit samar kay*' ('Akbar became curious about the peace and prosperity of Garha Mandla and Asaf Khan poisoned his mind and set forth with war drums beating'). Other modern Gondi songs also reference this appeal—in a 2020 song about the Veerangana by DJ Sarman, courage and competence go hand in hand: '*Garh Mandla raj chalaye Rani/Gondon ki laaj bachaye Rani/Mughlon se tu lari larai/Mughlon ko mar bhagai Rani*' ('The queen ran the kingdom of Garha Mandla and protected the honour of the Gond people; she battled the Mughals and drove them away').

Indeed a causal stroll around Jabalpur brings out this special appeal of the Veerangana. All modern-day representations of the queen have her dressed like a man, often wearing full mail armour, including a helmet, and astride her favourite elephant Sarman. In a sense, this depiction is not far from the truth—Durgawati would often wear the *jama* tunic with narrow trousers underneath, which was the common male attire in any sixteenth century court. Contemporary paintings show her in both sartorial avatars— the painting in Chennai Museum shows her in the skirt-bodice-shawl ensemble typical of the Rajput *poshak*. But the *Akbarnama* painting shows her clad in a printed jama tunic while on the battlefield.

But beyond administrative and military abilities, what also endeared the queen to her people was her benevolent nature. Durgawati had a formidable reputation for both scholarship and charity. Several contemporary sources highlight that her 'exalted qualities' and the kingdom's prosperity went hand in hand with the queen's prodigious reputation for charity. Just as she named lakes and tanks after both members of the royal family as well as senior ministers in her court, she similarly named villages both after her husband (Dalpatipur) and father-in-law (Amhanpur) as well as the Raj Purohit Mahesh Thakkur (Maheshpur). The Ramnagar inscription eulogizes this aspect of the queen: 'Durgavati, with her daily occupation, which consisted in unceasing donations of millions of horses, elephants, and pieces of gold, depreciated, in semblance, by her exalted celebrity, the universal honor of Kamadhenu.'[11] Other contemporary sources also talk about her 'good qualities'. Take *Samayalok*, which was written by Padmanabha Misra Bhattacharya, a poet who was part of Durgawati's court. The queen had in fact commissioned this treatise during her rule, but it remained incomplete after her defeat and death. *Samayalok* describes the queen as benevolent and full of excellent qualities: '*Dalapati nrpati preyasi kalpavallih ksonyam anya vadanyavadhir amalaguna bhati Durgavatiha*' ('Durgawati, the beloved of King Dalapati, was generous, benevolent and full of exalted qualities').[12]

Padmanabha Misra Bhattacharya was of course not the only literary figure to grace Durgawati's court. Apart from Mahesh Thakkur and Damodar Thakkur, whom she inherited from Dalpati Shah's time, the Garha court boasted several Sanskrit scholars, including Pandit Haridas, the author of *Prastab Ratnakar*, whom the queen appointed her son's personal tutor. Another family of poets who lived through the reigns of Dalpati Shah, Durgawati, Chandra Shah and Madhukar Shah were the Dixits—Anil Dixit, his son Vithal Dixit and grandson Keshav Dixit. Famed Vaishnav poet Kumbhandas, known for his 500-plus verses, was also a Garha resident for a while. Like Mahesh Thakkur, he too was invited to Akbar's court. Local lore says Man Singh wanted to gift Kumbhandas the village of Jamnawati, but the latter refused, saying that all he needed was the shade of a tree or two to sing about the Divine. This only increased Man Singh's admiration for the saintly man and was possibly how Akbar may have come to learn about him.

Garha's literary reputation was forged by two factors. First, several Raj Gond monarchs, including Sangram Shah and later Hirday Shah and Nizam Shah, were writers of repute themselves. Also, the tradition of welcoming Mythil Brahmins to Gondwana enriched Garha's literary renown, given that Mithila was the heart of Sanskrit learning in the Middle Ages. Garha also produced some excellent Hindi poetry during the time of the later Gonds, including works like *Sudamacharitra* and *Premdeepika*, written by Vir Bajpeyi in the late 1700s. While Sanskrit and Devanagari were the languages of scholarship in Garha, the common people mostly spoke Gondi with a smattering of Telugu and Maithili. Persian and Bundelkhandi influence was visible in official communiques.

Raj Gond sanads were typically written in Devanagari script, though their coins bear both Telugu and Devanagari imprints. Although the sanads invoked Lord Ram, Sangram Shah's patron deity was Bhyro or Shiv, and tantric worship was common in the region. As a Chandel princess, Durgawati's *kula devi* was Manaiya Devi, but after her marriage she set up both the Shiv temple on Barman Ghat in modern-day Narsinghpur and the Sharada Mata Mandir in Jabalpur. Krishna worship was also popular, as is evident from Dalpati Shah's land grant to the priest of a Radha Krishna temple in Rampur. Durga, Kali, Nag and Surya worship was also popular during the period.

The queen devoted a lot of time to sacred duties such as temple building, grants to holy men and fire sacrifices and *yajnas*. There is in fact a reference to a Bajpeyi yajna performed by Madhav Pathak in the *Gadhesh Nrpa Varnan Sangraha Slokah*. Written by poet Taresh, the sloka says this senior minister in Durgawati's court was the great-grandson of Sarve Pathak, who was the prime minister of Yadav Rai, the founder of the Raj Gond dynasty. The sloka also mentions that Pathak, like Adhar Kayastha or Man Brahmin, was another senior official Durgawati inherited from her husband's regime. Indeed Madhav Pathak had been in Garha right from Sangram Shah's time and was one of the oldest serving ministers in Durgawati's court.

As a prosperous and independent Hindu kingdom, Garha became a magnet for spiritual teachers of all dispensations. There are references to visits by several holy men during the reigns of Sangram Shah and later Durgawati. According to *Suraj Prakash*, the eighteenth-century text about Sikh Gurus, Guru Nanak visited Garha around the time Sangram Shah came to power and passed through the kingdom twice in the gap of two years, between 1508 and 1511. He criss-crossed the region, trekking from Odisha to Rewa to Amarkantak and later from Hoshangabad to Ujjain to Ramtek. The other holy teacher to visit Garha during Sangram Shah's rule was the Jain ascetic Taaran Taran Swamy, whose followers continue to live in central India to this day. As for Durgawati, the most well-known spiritual leader to visit her kingdom was Gusain Vitthalnath, the renowned Vallabh saint. Vitthalnath stopped in Garha en route from his tour of the south. Durgawati offered her respects as a devotee and donated 108 villages, which the holy man distributed among the Telang Brahmins who accompanied him from his southern tour. This incident was important enough to be remembered in literary traditions as well. Eighteenth-century Hindi poet Padmakar references it in his biography. According to him, 157 Panchdravid Dakshinatya Brahmins came to Garha in 1558 (Samvat 1615), at a time when the beautiful region on the banks of the Narmada was under Queen Durgawati: '*Ramye Narmada Koti Teerth militay Durgawati palitay*'. These southern Brahmins settled down in Garha, and Gusain Vitthalnath himself returned to the kingdom in 1563 on his way to Mathura.

He set up camp at Vishnutal, and the queen welcomed him once again with due respect. Immediately afterwards, the holy man married Padmavati in Garha. A description of this journey pops up in *Bhavsindhu*, a manuscript belonging to the Radhavallabha sect, the latter-day incarnation of the Gusain's Vallabh community of followers. Interestingly, like Mahesh Thakkur, Gusain/Goswami Vitthalnath is another name that connects Durgawati with Akbar. Vitthalnath and his father Acharya Vallabh were names that were taken with reverence in medieval India, and Vitthalnath had many admirers among sixteenth-century nobility, including Raja Todarmal, Raja Man Singh, Birbal, Tansen, Raja Ram Chandra and of course Rani Durgawati. Akbar himself was so impressed by the holy man's scholarship, his austere and saintly lifestyle and his exalted teachings that he made Gokul village in Govardhan pargana near Mathura tax free for the upkeep of the Srinath Temple. There are three or four firmans of the Mughal Emperor that mention Goswami Vitthalnath by name, offering him and his Vallabh community some privileges including allowing their cows to graze tax free all over Gokul and buying land for a temple and a cowshed.[13] Akbar's respect for both Mahesh Thakkur and Goswami Vitthalnath shows that despite its remoteness, the Mughal court was not entirely unaware of Garha and the riches—both in lucre and learning—that Durgawati's court boasted of.

That her people remember her reign as a golden age has as much to do with the learning and prosperity that the queen fostered as the political stability she ensured. A stability that was hard-fought, as we shall see.

8

War Drums at the Border

'Chandi roop dhari Maharani dono haath talwar'

(She is the very image of Goddess Chandi with swords in both hands)

—Gond folk song

One of the most abiding images of Rani Durgawati is the effortless way she embodies her celestial namesake on earth, particularly through her daredevilry on the battlefield. Durgawati is by no means an isolated example of India's time-honoured veerangana tradition. But she is a rare example of how an entire population deified their earthly queen on account of her valour. Gond folk songs have been singing about Rani Durgawati's bravery and sacrifice for the past nearly five centuries, and in every song, the queen and the goddess she was named after become interchangeable as patron-turned-protector. So entrenched is this cult of devotion that her samadhi *sthal* was, in fact, a place of worship until recently. According to Mandla historian Ram Bharosh Agarwal, right up until the mid-1950s, the samadhi of Rani

Durgawati used to receive '*diya-bati*' or lamp offerings from a resident *sevayat* or servitor called Amar Singh from the village Budra Pipriya, Bijadandi thana. Singh actually called himself 'Durgawati *ka sevak*' and offered regular prayers to an old and somewhat damaged murti of the rani as well as a Nag murti at the site.[1]

Of course, this reputation of the rani was hard fought. As regent of a prosperous kingdom surrounded by frosty if not openly hostile neighbours, Durgawati faced several skirmishes during her rule. One look at the political geography of Garha gives a clear picture of how precarious Durgawati's borders were. The queen had Ratanpur to the east, Raisen to the west, Panna in the north and the Baghels in the north east. Ratanpur was under the Haihai dynasty with Bahar Sahai on the throne. The Haihais never had good relations with the Raj Gonds, and it was Bahar Sahai's son and heir Kalyan Sahai who went to the Mughal court in 1563, just after Baz Bahadur's defeat against the Mughal army and just before Durgawati's final battle and death a year later. It can be reasonably assumed that Kalyan Sahai would have tried to win Akbar's support against any military ambitions that he may have suspected the rani to have been harbouring, now that Baz Bahadur was firmly out of the region's political equation.

To the south of Garha was the Gond kingdom of Chanda with Karn Shah at the helm. Since Durgawati's brother-in-law Chandra Shah had been offered asylum there, it can be assumed that Garha's relations with Chanda were not particularly warm. Southwest of Garha was Berar, which was under the Muslim rulers of Elichpur who controlled the fertile patch of land between the Kanhan and Wainganga rivers.

Northwest was Raisen, which, along with the rest of the fertile Malwa region, had been on the boil long before Durgawati became queen regent. A quick account of this region's tumultuous history gives some idea of how volatile things were. Back in 1492, this part of central India was under Gayasuddin, the Khalji king of Malwa. The Khaljis continued to rule this region for the next three-and-a-half decades or so, though by the time Mahmood II came along, real power had slipped out of the hands of the Khaljis and the king had become a puppet in the hands of powerful vassals. Mahmood, for instance, was more or less controlled by a feudal lord called Medini Rai who handed over Raisen, Bhilsa and Sarangpur to his brother Silhadi. In May 1532, Sultan Bahadur Shah of Gujarat—with some help from Durgawati's father-in-law Sangram Shah—captured Raisen, and Silhadi killed himself. Bahadur Shah, however, held on to his prize only for a short period. Just three years later, Humayun defeated Bahadur Shah, and Raisen and Chanderi were handed back to Silhadi's grandson Partab, who was under a guardian called Puranmal. In 1542, Sher Shah captured Raisen from Puranmal, Ujjain and Sarangpur from Qadir Shah and Seoni and Malwa from the Miyana Afghans led by Muin Khan and appointed Shujaat Khan as governor of the combined province. Malwa was under Shujaat Khan's son Baz Bahadur when Durgawati was at the helm in Garha. Given Baz Bahadur's attempts at military bullying, his feelings for Garha Mandla were clearly far from neighbourly.

Sher Shah's consolidation of Malwa also created another problem. The Miyana Afghans who had settled between Handia and Hoshangabad, mostly along the southern banks of the river Narmada, became leaderless after Muin Khan lost Seoni and Malwa to Sher Shah. This group then went around fomenting trouble in the region, instigating border skirmishes that Durgawati had to address and crush.[2] Of all her neighbours, only Baghel Raja Ram Chandra was friendly with Rani Durgawati. As an old ally of Sangram Shah and later Dalpati Shah, he did not molest Garha, though his misreading of the Mughal interest in central Indian kingdoms did cost both him, and by extension Durgawati, dear.

Garha's geopolitical landscape shows that Durgawati was surrounded by baying jackals. But as long as Mughal power stayed away from that equation, she managed to keep her neighbours in check through some deft political steps as well as military muscle-flexing, as we shall see. According to Abul Fazl, Durgawati faced two major military challenges before Asaf Khan and emerged victorious in both of them. But thanks to the region's complex skein of political ambition, both these battles, and their fallout, severely affected the future of not just Durgawati but Baz Bahadur as well.

Durgawati's trouble with Baz Bahadur started with the Miyana Afghans. A section of this tribe from the Bhopal region decided to side with Ibrahim Shah Suri in the game of thrones that followed Sher Shah's death. Their combined forces marched against Baz Bahadur. Durgawati, who had been watching the political scenario unfold around her after Sher Shah's death, decided to back Ibrahim. Baz Bahadur, scared that the delicate political balance in the region was tilting away from him, then sent ambassadors to the queen's court to convince her that this was not her battle to fight. The rani, who may well have been only posturing, saw the logic in what Baz Bahadur was saying and withdrew her forces from the confederation. With Garha out of the equation, the fight went out of the Miyana Afghans, and Ibrahim Shah Suri proceeded on to Odisha, which is where he finally died, a couple of years after the battle of Narai. This little political footwork, though caused the rani more trouble than it was worth. First, it must have seriously angered Baz Bahadur, prompting him to attack her later. For another, one break-away faction of the Miyanas also attacked Garha, though they were firmly defeated by Durgawati. Following the drubbing, however, many Miyana Afghan generals joined Durgawati's army, and some of them, including the likes of Shams Khan Miyana, Mubarak Khan, Khan Jahan Ukib and Bukhari Rumi, rose to prominence in Garha.

Baz Bahadur's misadventure against the rani could well have its roots in the incident involving Ibrahim Suri. Although, like many others, he would have considered Garha, a rich kingdom ruled by a woman, low-hanging fruit. Baz Bahadur attacked Garha the same year that Akbar became emperor—1556. A teenage Mughal emperor surrounded by power-hungry courtiers was not much of a deterrent and, with the Suris and Mughals on the war-path, a regional ruler like Baz Bahadur realized he had enough elbow room to try out some local military arm-flexing. What followed however was something he had trouble living down.

In his *History of the Rise of the Mahomedan Power in India*,[3] contemporary chronicler Mahomed Kasim Ferishta

gives an extremely detailed and very colourful account of
Baz Bahadur's humiliating defeat in the hands of Durgawati.
Baz Bahadur first attacked Garha but lost so many men in
the skirmish, including senior generals and family members,
that he had to turn back. 'He marched to invade Gondwana
in which campaign his uncle Futteh Khan was killed; after
which he returned to Sarangpur and made preparations to
reduce the fortress of Garha,' writes Ferishta.[4]

But the rani cleverly decided to use the rugged terrain
to her advantage and lured Baz Bahadur and his men into a
mountain pass ambush that was both brutal and decisive. Her
army did not have canons, but the Gonds were expert archers
and knew the terrain like the back of their hands. This is what
the rani used to her advantage. She chose a narrow pass and
forced Baz Bahadur to attack in a single file. Gond archers
were already positioned all along the course, and once the
charge began, Gond infantry and archers made mincemeat of
the invading army. The terrain allowed Durgawati to mount
attacks both on the front as well as the rear of the enemy
force. Baz Bahadur's overconfidence and battle-frenzy did
not allow him to think clearly enough and see the trap he was
leading his men into, particularly since an earlier skirmish
had also gone against him. Ferishta as usual gives the details.
'On his arrival in the vicinity he was opposed by the troops
of Rani Durgawati . . . who governed the country,' he writes.

> Baz Bahadur was opposed by the Gonds on the summit
> of a pass where their infantry was strong posted and
> having been drawn into an ambushcade his troops were
> so completely routed that he was compelled to make his

escape singly to Sarangpur; but his army was completely
surrounded and made prisoners, most of them were put
to death.

This decisive victory against a powerful neighbour was an
important point in the rani's career as regent. She started the
tradition of planting a wish-fulfilling pennant at the Sharada
Mata Mandir near Madan Mahal after this victory—a
tradition that continues to this day. She later also tried to
replicate the exact same strategy in the biggest battle of her life
and once again achieved remarkable success. These back-to-
back military victories earned her the respect of contemporary
historians, including Abul Fazl, who admitted that Durgawati
'neglected no point of courage or capacity, and did great things
by dint of her farseeing abilities. She had great contests with
Baz Bahadur and the Miyanas, and was always victorious'.[5]
Local lore claims that Durgawati faced as many as fifty-one
battles and remained unvanquished. This could be history
covered in hyperbole. Given how hostile her neighbourhood
was, it is entirely possible that the rani faced a number of
minor skirmishes throughout her reign and contemporary
chroniclers only recorded the three major ones.

The praise that Durgawati earned from her contemporaries
was a double-edged sword—along with it came jealousy.
As long as the Mughal court was in turmoil, her neighbours
watched Durgawati with hawk-eyed interest and jealous respect.
The moment Akbar came into his own, they tried to win his
protection against what they saw as a dominant neighbour.

Durgawati probably sensed the danger of neighbours
snitching about her to Akbar. For someone who was as astute

in realpolitik as she was, it was unthinkable that she did not see the resentment building up around her. Indeed, she may even have tried her hand at diplomacy: Apart from lavish gifts for the two Mughal officials who visited her court, she would have tried to use her ablest minister to secure a peace deal for her kingdom. Local historians, including Suresh Mishra and Ram Bharosh Agarwal, say Adhar Kayastha's legendary trip to the Mughal durbar was probably backed by a subtle political agenda—the minister was to secure a promise from the young emperor that Garha Mandla would not be attacked by him. As it turns out, for all his dazzling wit, this was a mission that Kayastha clearly did not succeed in.

As for Baz Bahadur, this walloping at the hands of a neighbour and a woman would have been a bitter pill to swallow and he, very melodramatically, sought solace in wine and song. Ferishta says Baz Bahadur was 'so much affected with this disgraceful termination of the war in which his army had been destroyed without being able to make resistance that in order to drive away care he abandoned himself to sensual pleasures'. If that sounds almost textbook Bollywood, remember too that he left his legendary paramour Rupmati to suicide after the Mughal army defeated him 7 years later. All of which only proves the point that an *aashiq* who wears his heart and song on his sleeve may not necessarily be a trustworthy partner.

Baz Bahadur's humiliation wasn't unexpected given how much importance the Raj Gond queen gave to border security. Durgawati's efforts to add muscle to her armed forces started with refurbishing the fortress-garhs in her rugged kingdom and moving the capital to the truly inaccessible Chauragarh

Fort. Just how important she considered fortress rebuilds becomes clear from the fact that her garhs are mentioned in multiple contemporary sources. The *Prastab Ratnakar*, commissioned by the queen herself, leaves one in no doubt about the importance of fortresses in strategic defence. There are various types of *durgs* or forts, says the book[6]—'on high mountains, in a water body, surrounded by a moat or high walls. The job that cannot be done by thousands and lakhs of elephants can be accomplished by a fortified stronghold'. The Ramnagar inscription seconds that view, saying that the fortresses under Sangram Shah were 'indestructible' because they 'possessed the firm strength of mountains'. Given her focus on terrain warfare, Durgawati would have realized the importance of inaccessible forts with their own water supplies only too well. In fact, that focus on fort building continued to attract the historian's gaze to the Raj Gond dynasty long after Durgawati's final sacrifice. Three centuries after the Battle of Narai, in his *Highlands of Central India*, James Forsyth writes[7] that the 'hilltop forts of the Satpura mountains' were 'inaccessible' and the last disintegrating vestiges of Raj Gond glory lay in these 'crumbling' forts and ramparts. 'Mandla was at one time the seat of one of the Gond-Rajput ruling dynasties,' he writes, 'and the remains of their forts and other buildings still crown, in crumbling decay, the top of many a forest-covered mound.'[8]

Apart from defence infrastructure, the queen also further decentralized her army, a system that placed a large chunk of the responsibility of maintaining the soldiers on feudal lords. As discussed before, the Gond state largely retained its tribal sensibilities and was, therefore, more decentralized in its power structure than neighbouring kingdoms. The king retained direct control over some villages, but the rest of the land was divided into garhs or fortress districts controlled by local lords. In times of war, these feudal lords participated in any military action ordered by the Raj Gond king or queen and fought under the Raj Gond banner of the rampaging horned tiger grabbing an elephant. The garrisons were primarily led by and so were loyal to their feudal lords and more prone to deserting the battlefield if the tide turned against them. The Gond soldiers trained with bow and arrow, swords and spears—weapons that they would normally use for hunting, for instance. They did not get any special training in military formation, nor did the Gond army have cannons. That her army managed to repulse multiple attacks from hostile neighbours despite these drawbacks speaks volumes of the queen's personal charisma, the loyalty of her top generals and the bravery of the Gond rank and file. Unfortunately, the decentralized structure of the armed forces allowed Gond feudal lords far more say in military decision-making than should have been allowed. As a result, the queen's decisions were repeatedly overruled by her commanders in the heat of the battle, which had a domino effect on both the kingdom and the dynasty.

To her credit, the queen did everything she could to ensure that the gourd of Garha remained secure during her reign. Some of the decisions she took were clearly out of the box, even though she did not sometimes get the support of the men around her to follow them through. Local historians say, for instance, that there are bardic references to the fact that the queen started a separate regiment of women soldiers.

The women's corps was headed by her trusted friend Ram Cheri (who also had a lake named after her near Jabalpur), and this division was directly under the supervision of the queen herself.[9] There are no contemporary references to this veerangana brigade, however, though that does not necessarily prove that the women's corps did not exist. Indeed they could well have formed an essential part of the capital's defence strategy, with the rani herself leading from the front. The Ramnagar inscription describes her as forever battle ready: 'Mounted on an elephant, in person, and by force overmastering, in many a battle, prepotent adversaries, ever studious for the safeguard of her subjects, she superseded, to all appearance, the protectors of the regions.'[10] This is how Durgawati is remembered even today with statues and memorials showing her in full chain mail armour, sword unsheathed and mounted atop her favourite elephant Sarman. And this is exactly how she appeared to her biggest adversary—Mughal general Asaf Khan.

9

—Pen, Power and Perfidy: Khwaja Abdul Majid Asaf Khan

'Naam Asaf dushmon kay'

(The enemy is called Asaf Khan)

—Gond folk song

There is delicate irony in the fact that both the aggressor and the defender in the tragic story of Veerangana Durgawati have been frozen in paint, their most defining moments carefully detailed with colour and imagination in that time-capsule called the *Akbarnama*. In a wonderfully evocative painting by Mughal artists Miskina and Bhagwan, Khwaja Abdul Majid Asaf Khan is shown offering tributes to his emperor Akbar in Jaunpur, his body language displaying extreme deference and humility. That bent-back *kornish* and the servility it symbolized was far from heartfelt though. This was the summer of 1565, and Asaf Khan was flush with success after his recent victory on the battlefield. Yet by this time, he was by no means confident of either his master's trust in him or his own loyalty to the Mughal crown. What he did subsequently further widened the rift between Akbar and this once-trusted noble.

So who was this tall, lean, pale, white-turbaned man, offering to Akbar what looks like spoils of war? And why was this very public display of fealty so awash with the irony that was often the after-effect of dizzying ambition in medieval times? According to Abul Fazl, Khwaja Abdul Majid was a Persian-speaking Tajik who belonged to the 'writing class' (as opposed to the sword-wielding Turk). He was 'raised from the *qalam* (pen) to the *saif* (sword) and had joined those who wear both the sword and the pen and are masters both of war and of peace'.[1]

Abul Fazl goes on to suggest that Abdul Majid rose rapidly in the early years of Akbar's reign because he was smart enough to grab the opportunities that a fast-expanding empire offered. 'By being supported by the dominion which is conjoined with eternity he did deeds which made Turks humble themselves before him,' says Fazl.[2] Although that off-the-cuff introduction makes him sound like a Johnny-come-lately sword-for-hire, the reality of Abdul Majid was a little more nuanced. This Mughal general actually boasted a well-known lineage, and some of his ancestors enjoyed a long association with Akbar's family that went back several generations. According to the *Maathir-ul-umara*,[3] Majid was descended from Shaikh Abu Bakr Taibadi, who of course had a near-mythical meeting with Amir Timur going back to 1380–81. That was the year Timur attacked and wrested the city of Herat from the Kartid ruler Ghiyassuddin. The story goes that after the city fell, Timur demanded an explanation from Taibadi, asking him why he did not come and pay his respects to the new ruler of Herat. The wise man replied, 'What have I to do with you?' Taken aback, Timur quizzed him further: 'Why did you not advise Ghiyassuddin better?' To which Taibadi said, 'I did but he did not listen. God has sent you against him, I now advise you to be just.' The legend then says that this calm honesty in the face of almost certain death impressed Amir Timur enormously, prompting him to comment: 'During my Sultanate with whatever darvish I consorted I perceived that each of them was in his heart thinking about himself except the Shaikh whom I found separated from himself or *min khudra dar hajab*.'[4]

History does not tell us much about what happened to the intervening generations of Abdul Majid's family. Like the mix-up between Keerat Singh and Shalivahan in Durgawati's family tree, there is some confusion about Abdul Majid as well because the *Iqbalnama* mentions that he was descended from Raknud-din-Khwafi and that he was originally from Merv in central Asia. Either way, he grew up in Herat (in modern-day Afghanistan) and first popped up on the Mughal radar as a young recruit in the service of Humayun's brother Askari in Kandahar. Majid was clearly ambitious and hard-working, which is why he would have caught Humayun's eye, enough to not only find employment but also subsequent favour. Humayun quickly promoted him to the position of diwan, even as he readied himself to take back the throne of Hind from Sher Shah Suri's descendants.

According to Abul Fazl, twenty-one Irani nobles accompanied Humayun on his India campaign. These included some senior officials like Bairam Khan; Afzal

Khan, who was Mir Bakshi; Ashraf Khan, who was Mir Munshi; Khwaja Ataullah, who was Diwan-i-Bayutat; Mir Shahbuddin, who was Mir Saman, among others. Khwaja Abdul Majid's name crops up on this list as Humayun's diwan. However, a more detailed list of Humayun's nobles come from Abul Fazl's contemporary Bayazid Bayat. In his *Tazkira-i-Humayun wa Akbar*, Bayazid refers to Khwaja Abdul Majid with the work-title Mustaufi,[5] or accountant. Clearly, Majid did get a quick promotion or two before the Indian campaign. The *Maathir-ul-umara* describes his ascent succinctly: 'Khwaja Abdul Majid was one of the servants of Humayun and on account of his honesty and skill he was made Diwan at the time of the conquest of India.'[6]

Five years later, history would repeat itself. Just as his father picked Abdul Majid for an important responsibility before riding out to re-claim his destiny, so too would Akbar. To the young Akbar, a senior official appointed by his father was clearly an important administrative asset given how surrounded he was in his initial years by those who tried to control him and the power that emanated from his position. Not surprisingly, Abdul Majid's rise and rise continued particularly in the wake of Bairam Khan's fall from grace as Akbar headed out to encounter his mentor-turned-enemy. That's when the emperor entrusted Delhi to the care of Abdul Majid and conferred on his father's retainer the title of Asaf Khan. 'When the world renewed its youth by accession of Akbar, the Khwaja was exalted from the Diwani to the rank of commander (Sirdari) and united the sword with the pen,' says the *Maathir-ul-umara*. 'When Akbar proceeded to the Punjab in connection with the affair of Bairam Khan, the

Khwaja got the title of Asaf Khan and acquired reputation as governor of Delhi.' Abul Fazl, characteristically, sees in this appointment proof of how good a judge of character his emperor was: 'When in his perfect foresight His Majesty determined to make the expedition he, for the purpose of carrying on the affairs of the state, exalted Khwajah Abdul Majid who had been made Sarif-Diwani by conferring on him the title Asaf Khan and he assigned to him the government of Delhi as part of the office of Vizier.'

The job and the responsibility that came with it was nothing new for Majid. He had already been appointed Sarif-Diwani by Humayun and, as such, would have been well aware of what the role demanded. But to be left in charge of the 'affairs of the state' in the emperor's absence would have been heady indeed. The new role was not only important, it came with its own trappings of power. 'He received a drum and a flag and an office of 3000,' says the *Maathir-ul-umara*. That these 'kingly admonitions' were dazzling enough to give an ambitious man delusions of grandeur was a prospect not lost on Akbar. Abul Fazl in fact chronicles the words of wisdom that these perks of power came with. 'He [Akbar] bade him [Abdul Majid] not to be proud of his own wisdom and dignity, to remember the favours he had received and to regard his exaltation as involved in his humility and to consider His Majesty's grace as the reward of his services and to withhold his eye, his heart, his hand and his tongue from men's goods.'[7] In short, the emperor warned Majid not to get ideas above his station.

The warning worked. From all accounts, Majid, now called by his new title Asaf Khan, understood what was expected of him. 'The Khwajah understood the precious monitions and illuminated his auspicious forehead by prostrating it on the sublime threshold,' writes Abul Fazl. 'He gave his heart to his work and exerted himself sincerely and devotedly.'

Abul Fazl was right in a sense. One reason why Abdul Majid rose so quickly was because he was at the right place at the right time. Alongside Turani (central Asian) officials, Iranis (Persians) formed a dominant bloc in the Mughal court, so an Irani noble chosen by Humayun would have quickly found favour with Akbar. Also, after the overthrow of Bairam Khan, Akbar faced rebellion in his ranks mostly from Turani and Uzbek nobles. Between 1562 and 1567, the young Mughal monarch faced six uprisings and desertions. Abdul Majid was the only Irani name on that roster of dubious distinction. Akbar promoted several Irani nobles who were either working for Humayun or under Bairam Khan around this time, and Majid was one of them. He went from 3,000 to 5,000 horse in three years, was appointed governor of Kurra Manikpur and, five years later, Chittor. And despite his questionable loyalty, he was included in the devastating siege of Chittorgarh in 1567–68. Akbar also repeatedly forgave his transgressions as he did with many of the other Irani generals in his service.

As for the perks-with-warning that greeted Khwaja Abdul Majid's elevation to the title of Asaf Khan, this too was entirely in character for the emperor. Akbar sent out a similar cautionary message to his foster brother Adham Khan (son of Maham Anaga) before leaving for the stare-down with Bairam Khan. Akbar told Adham Khan that while he was leaving Bairam Khan's protégé Husain Quli Beg in his charge in Delhi, if anything were to happen to Beg, he would hold Adham Khan personally responsible. It's not that Akbar was particularly enamoured of Husain Quli Beg at this point. In fact, he felt that Beg had been promoted out-of-turn due to nepotism. In his farman dismissing Bairam Khan, Akbar actually grumbles that Khan 'gave Husain Quli who has not even fought with a chicken, equal position with Iskandar Khan'.[8] This was two years before Adham Khan was summarily chucked off the terrace twice over for his greed and perfidy, so the warning bells should already have been ringing loud and clear. It is an early indication that Akbar knew exactly how far to trust his milk brother or anybody else for that matter.

Interestingly, Adham Khan and Asaf Khan experienced identical 'slings and arrows' of fortune in central India. Adham Khan's conquest of Malwa and the booty it offered up—even though Baz Bahadur's beautiful consort Rupmati chose suicide rather than surrender—verily turned his head, prompting him to keep the larger share of the loot for himself. It was when Akbar pursued and accosted him that Adham Khan coughed up what he had pilfered. Asaf Khan did the same after the fall of Garha, as the painting in the *Akbarnama* shows in such detail.

As for Asaf Khan, just how efficient was he as governor of Delhi, particularly in controlling entrenched corruption in the system? In his seminal book *The Agrarian System of Moslem India*, W.H. Moreland translates a passage from *Ain-i-Dahsala*, which gives a glimpse of how things were around the 1560s.

> When Khwaja Abdul Majid Asaf Khan was Vazir, the *jama-i-wilayat* (valuation) was *raqami* (arbitrary) and they used to show whatever they pleased with the pen of enhanced salary. Seeing that the kingdom was not extensive and that promotion of officers used to be frequent, there used to be increase and decrease from bribe taking and self-interest.[9]

Whatever his merits as an imperial officer, corruption continued unabated under Asaf Khan's governorship. The *Ain* also mentions how things changed when the 'supreme office [the *vazarat*] fell to Muzaffar Khan and Raja Todar Mal in the 15th year' and a 'new *jama* came into force'.[10]

Administrative duties aside, Asaf Khan did, however, acquit himself reasonably well on the battlefield. Between 1561 and 1564, his name comes up in connection with two expeditions—the submission of Chunar Fort and the campaign against Panna. Abul Fazl says the first of these two campaigns was more of a diplomatic rather than a military affair. 'When the standards of fortune returned from the town of Karra and were set down at Agra, Abdul Majid Asaf Khan was appointed to take the fort of Chunar,' says the *Akbarnama*.[11] The fort was important because it was inaccessible and almost impossible to storm or siege. But the sight of the Mughal contingent clearly unnerved the incongruously named Fattu, the man in charge of the fort. So he put forth his terms for surrender: As long as the Sufi saint Muhammad Ghawth 'were to take him by the hand and bring him to kiss the threshold of fortune he would assuredly deliver the fort with a contented mind to the imperial servants'. His petition was accepted, and

Akbar appointed Hasan Ali Khan Turkaman in charge of the fortress.

The expedition to Panna was a bit more complicated. The year was 1561. A rebellious Afghan noble called Ghazi Khan Tanuri had taken refuge in the kingdom of Bhatta or Rewa ruled by Baghel king Ram Chandra. Akbar's orders were clear: If the Raja gave up Tanuri and some of the other rebels he was harbouring in his kingdom, Asaf Khan was not to molest him in any way. Abul Fazl as usual gives a detailed account of what happened. 'At this time Abdul Majid was sent off with a number of warriors towards Pannah against Rajah Ram Chand,' he writes. 'If he behaved properly, and seized and sent to court Ghazi Khan Tanuri and a number of broken men who had gone to that country, and if he himself bound on the girdle of obedience and good service, they were to return after having treated him in a conciliatory fashion.'[12] Asaf Khan did as he was told and sent out the imperial message to the raja, who refused to give up the rebels. Initially this led to a stand-off. 'As it was the rainy season, the Rajah was obstinate and the holy warriors returned and went to their fiefs,' says Fazl.[13]

The *Maathir-ul-Umara* gives a detailed account of what happened thereafter. The raja of Panna, 'in his presumptuousness, joined with those wretches [Ghazi Khan Tanuri and other assorted rebels] and prepared for war. Asaf Khan behaved with energy and killed the refugees. The Rajah was defeated and took refuge in the fortress of Bandhu which was the strongest fortress in that country'. At this point, several rajas acceded on his behalf to Akbar and Raja Ram Chandra himself decided to give in. 'As last by agreeing to make submission and the intercession of the Rajahs who were near Akbar, an order was issued to Asaf Khan to abstain from attaching the Rajah. Asaf therefore withdrew.'[14] If the Baghel king harboured any illusions about Akbar remembering his family's history with Vir Bhanu, this campaign must have speedily disabused him.

The fall of Panna was important for two reasons: first, because it brought the Mughal empire to Durgawati's doorstep. By 1563, Asaf Khan had wrangled another promotion and was now a noble of 5,000 horses. He was also in charge of 'Kurra Manikpoor' and, therefore, dangerously close to Durgawati's borders. Also, Asaf Khan's success in the Panna campaign made him greedy for more battles and booty. 'As he had acquired so much power by his victory [over the Raja of Panna], he formed the idea of conquering Garha,' says the *Maathir-ul-Umara*.[15] Cunningham dittos this, writing, 'reports of her [Durgawati's] wealth excited the cupidity of Asaf Khan'.[16] What happened in the next year or so would not only destroy Garha but also result in the near-complete destruction of the Raj Gond royal line, with the exception of Durgawati's estranged brother-in-law Chandra Shah. In a sense, the Battle of Narai Nala was the culmination of a series of events that began with the invasion of Malwa by Akbar's forces.

Gond folk songs are very clear about what they think of the man who brought their proud and prosperous kingdom to its knees. '*Naam Asaf dushmon kay, gayish dhari dhari haar/ Saj dhaj kaya ave tisariya, fauji dharey hathiyar*' ('The enemy is called Asaf Khan, and he lost his battle as the men of Garha wore their war gear and picked up their weapons'),[17] goes the song, calling Asaf Khan 'the enemy' and describing how the Mughal forces were beaten back several times before the final confrontation at Narai. More modern songs, place the blame of the attack itself squarely on Asaf Khan, holding him responsible for poisoning Akbar's ears about Rani Durgawati. In these versions, Akbar is the gullible sovereign and Asaf Khan the snake in his backyard. Respected poet Acharya Bhagwat Dubey's famous song about Durgawati explores this angle: '*Kaan bhar kay Akbar ke Asaf Khan chal paro/Nagare pit samar kay*' ('Asaf Khan poisoned Akbar's mind and set forth with war drums beating'). That Asaf Khan was as eager to take his war drums to Garha as Akbar was is obvious. But the power-politics between master and servant was probably a bit more nuanced.

Interestingly the Ramnagar inscription in Mandla whitewashes this invasion and turns it into a routine tax raid. The inscription, dated to the reign of Hirday Shah or Hirde Shah in the mid-seventeenth century, says that Asaf Khan came to Garha to collect taxes. Fitz Edward Hall's translation of the inscription is telling: 'Asaf Khan, with an army, was deputed by King Akbar, Puruhuta of the earth, all but compeer of Partha, for the purpose of levying a contribution.'[18] Just as Akbar is likened to Arjuna in this panegyric, Asaf Khan is described as a 'great warrior—a Bhima in prowess, whose armaments depressed the face of the earth'. The political spin is understandable, given that the inscription came nearly 100 years after the Battle of Narai Nala, during the reign of Hirday Shah, who had more or less cordial relations with the Mughal emperor of the time, Shah Jahan. Hirday Shah in fact sought and received help

from Shah Jahan when he was ousted from Chauragarh by
Bundela Raja Jujhar Singh, though the Mughal emperor was
more angered by Jujhar's refusal to pay the hefty penalty he
demanded rather than moved by the Gond king's plight. Be
that as it may, Hirday Shah had very good reasons for not
wanting to spoil his relations with the Mughals. That local
memory has continued to despise Asaf Khan for more than
four centuries despite such attempts at official revisionism is
no less extraordinary.

Painting Asaf Khan as the villain of the piece is easily done.
As a character from the pages of history, he starts out as an
ambitious imperial officer but ends up looking more and more
like a self-serving profiteer. His conquest of Garha turned
out to be both his biggest boon and bane, colouring the way
posterity will always remember him. Contemporary historians
are absolutely scathing about the real purpose behind the
campaign and Asaf Khan's subsequent treachery against Akbar.
Referencing Abul Fazl, Ferishta makes it very clear that it was
greed for gold that drove Asaf Khan to Garha: 'Asuf Khan
Hirvy heard of the riches of this country, and visited with
constant depredations, till at length he marched with a force of
between five and six thousand cavalry to Gurra.'[19]

While there's really not much that can be said to
redeem Asaf Khan, the reality of the Garha conquest was
probably a lot less black-and-white. As an official appointed
by Humayun, Khwaja Abdul Majid would have enjoyed a
certain degree of closeness with Akbar. Like he forgave the
treachery and trespasses of so many of his noblemen—Bairam
Khan included—Akbar also pardoned Asaf Khan twice over
and restored him to favour. But, as we have discussed before,

no matter how persuasive Asaf Khan may have been and how much Akbar valued his counsel as his father's retainer, the final decision to attack Garha was firmly backed by imperial command. Ferishta's account says as much: 'When Asuf Khan was raised to the rank of a noble of five thousand horse, and procured the government of Kurra Manikpoor, he obtained permission of the king to subdue a country called Gurra, at that time governed by a Rany whose name was Durgawutty.' Akbar, for his own reasons, wanted this part of the country under his control. The decision to go after Durgawati had his seal of approval. Asaf Khan was the means to an end, not the reason for it.

The Battle of Narai Nala, or the Battle of Damoh, as some sources refer to the attack on Garha, will feature prominently elsewhere in this narrative, so it will be interesting at this point to see what happened just before and after the fall of Durgawati and the young Bir Narayan. Even before he formally waged war against Garha, Asaf Khan had been trying to intimidate Rani Durgawati with frequent border raids. A rich kingdom ruled by a woman was, for him, just too juicy a bait to ignore. Contemporary historian Khwaja Nizamuddin Ahmad explains Asaf Khan's motivations in the *Tabaqat-i-Akbari*: 'As the country of Garha Katinka was close to the place of government of Asaf Khan, a desire to conquer that country entered his head.'[20] Like a seasoned campaigner, Asaf Khan sent his men to check out the lay of the land. Garha's biggest protection was its terrain and the inaccessibility of its forts, particularly the capital Chauragarh. 'Asaf Khan ascertained by means of spies the modes of access to the country,' says the *Maathir-ul-Umara*.[21]

The reports his spies brought back convinced Asaf Khan that Garha was low-hanging fruit, waiting to be plucked. 'The capital of that country is the fort of Chauragarh and it is an extensive territory having 70,000 cultivated villages,' says the *Tabaqat-i-Akbari*. 'The ruler of this country at that time was a woman named Rani Dugawati. When Asaf Khan received information about the truth of that country, the conquest of it appeared to be easy in the eye of his spirit and energy.'[22]

His military successes, first against the king of Panna and then against Durgawati and Bir Narayan, went to Asaf Khan's head though. Every single contemporary historian clearly mentions how the riches from the sack of Chauragarh fort, described in detail in Chapter 2, started giving him delusions of grandeur. The *Maathir-ul-Umara* tells us how it happened. 'Asaf Khan set off to seize Churagarha which was a fort and a capital and had many buried treasures . . . After this victory, which was the greatest of Asaf Khan's achievements, he became possessed of boundless treasures and grew proud and arrogant. He went astray . . .'[23]

Asaf Khan may have been dreaming impossible dreams, but for the emperor and the court, his victory was simply the result of his good fortune of being on the winning side. Abul Fazl, for instance, gives equal credit for the Garha victories to God and good luck. 'Asaf Khan by his excellent service, loyalty and reliance upon the eternal dominion was divinely favoured and conquered the territory of Garha,' he writes.[24]

Meanwhile Asaf Khan, having secured for himself what he thought was a rich and remote bolt-hole, continued in Garha for the next one year, sending back to his emperor only 200 out of the 1,000 elephants that were part of the huge treasure he captured at Chauragarh. From June 1564 to July 1565, he remained in Garha, perhaps harbouring hopes of breaking free from the imperial hold.

In the end, though, it was the antics of a fellow noble that put paid to his plans. According to the *Ain*, yet another insurrection by the tirelessly mutinous Khan Zaman (Ali Quli Khan) brought Akbar to Jaunpur in hot pursuit, and Asaf Khan, wisely realizing the emperor was way too close by for comfort, came with '5000 troopers' and 'handed over the remainder of the Garha spoils' to his master.[25] It is this moment that is captured in the painting by Miskina and Bhagwan, which explains the complex body language on display. What happened next justifies the unease that shines through in the painting. Another painting by Miskina and Nanha, also from the *Akbarnama*, shows Asaf Khan in Akbar's company, with a parade of elephants in the background, underlining that Akbar was far from amused by the way Asaf Khan withheld the Garha treasure in general and the famed elephants in particular.

Asaf Khan's grovelling and the emperor's confidence in him—he was asked to hunt down the rebels—did not last long though. Abul Fazl suggests, with his usual flowery flourish, that a guilty conscience made Asaf Khan more susceptible to rumour than he should have been, and he simply ran away. 'Asaf Khan, out of haste and volatility, committed an act whose shamefulness could not be removed by the labours of all the writers in the world,' writes Abul Fazl, bristling with censure and indignation.

Though the graciousness of the Shahinshah pardoned those faults and so cleansed the cheek of shame from the

> dust of crime, yet the mark of them remained . . . Asaf
> Khan, who after having been appointed to high office
> had lately been honoured by the command of a victorious
> army, had, owing to the fact that fear attaches to the skirt
> of the perfidious, been carried away by the tale-bearings
> of strife-mongers, and had disregarded the preservation of
> his position, and from a vain terror fled to Garha.[26]

Abul Fazl is clear that the reason Asaf Khan lost his nerve had
as much to do with court politics as with his own guilt and fear.
Asaf Khan, he says, 'had basely and ungratefully concealed
them [Garha treasures] from his king and benefactor, by whose
favour he had been advanced from the pen to the standard
az qalm-b-'ilm [from pen to panoply] thereby prepared the
materials of his own downfall.' Asaf Khan, like many imperial
officials, had been generously bribing the imperial *mutasaddis*
or clerks, which made matters worse for him because these
'covetous ones' were 'always uttering dark hints'. When he
submitted his army to Akbar and was 'treated with royal
favours, the grandees were moved to envy'. Bayazid, as usual,
has another angle to this story. According to him, Asaf Khan
lost his nerve when Muzaffar Khan began enquiries about the
Garha treasure. Finally, says Fazl, on Sunday, 16 September
1565, 'he left his tents and goods and went off to Garha with
his brother Wazir'.

Akbar would have been furious with this volte face.
According to Abul Fazl, the emperor immediately sent
Shujaat Khan to pursue Asaf. Shujaat arrived at Manikpur
and 'learned that he [Asaf Khan] had reached Karra and
was preparing to go to Garha'. At this point, the two had

a furious clash. Shujaat had procured some boats and was contemplating crossing a river. 'On the other side Asaf Khan got information of the coming of Shujaat Khan and turned back with his army in order to stop him on the riverbank.' When Shujaat's boats were near the shore, Asaf Khan attacked. 'A hot engagement took place between him [Asaf Khan] and the troops who were in the boats.' By all accounts, it was an intense battle, with a hail of 'arrows and bullets' rending the air. But by end of day, Asaf Khan realized flight was 'his best resource'. The next morning, Shujaat saw that his target had disappeared and came to the conclusion that 'it would be exceedingly difficult to reach him'. So he turned around and returned to Jaunpur.[27]

Asaf Khan may have avoided an encounter with imperial forces, but the Garha treasure continued to haunt him, and he remained a fugitive till 1566. And then panic and greed made him take absolutely the worst decision of his life. When Mahdi Qasim Khan was appointed as the new governor of Garha, Akbar gave him clear instructions: 'he was to administer the territory and to arrest Asaf Khan who had perpetrated so much wickedness', writes Abul Fazl. 'Mahdi Qasim Khan girded up the loins of resolution and set out, but before his army arrived, Asaf Khan got information and with much regret left the country. He became a wanderer in the fields of wretchedness and, like a wild beast, took refuge in the forests.'[28]

Hunted by Mahdi Qasim, Asaf Khan turned to Khan Zaman Ali Quli in the classic logic of an enemy's enemy being a friend. According to the *Maathir-ul-Umara*, 'Asaf Khan left with many regrets that country and with his brother

Wazir Khan accepted an invitation from the Khan Zaman
and joined him in Jaunpur.' But as soon as he joined the
rebels, Asaf Khan realized this was a big mistake—what Khan
Zaman Ali Quli really wanted was the Garha treasure. The
Maathir says as much: 'On the first interview he perceived
the Khan Zaman's tyranny and arrogance and repented of
his coming. And when he saw his cupidity was excited by his
possessions, he sought an opportunity of leaving him.'[29]

Khan Zaman detained Wazir Khan and asked Asaf Khan
to join his own brother Bahadur Khan in a raid against the
Afghans. What happened next could put the best screen
chase sequences to shame. Asaf Khan managed to slip away,
and Wazir Khan also escaped. Both brothers made for a
spot in Manikpur which was their appointed rendezvous
point. But Bahadur Khan, who was probably expecting this,
gave chase and took Asaf Khan prisoner. 'Bahadur's men
immediately dispersed in search of plunder when suddenly
Wazir Khan fell over Bahadur. Bahadur made someone a
sign to kill Asaf who sat fettered on an elephant and Asaf
had received a wound in his hand and nose when Wazir
saved his life and carried him away.'[30] How badly was Asaf
Khan wounded? The *Tabaqat* says three of his fingers were
chopped off. Relentlessly hunted, grievously injured and
now totally friendless, the brothers finally came to their
senses. By late 1566, Asaf and Wazir decided that it was
better to grovel once more for an imperial pardon. They
reached Karra and requested Muzaffar Khan to intercede on
their behalf. Muzaffar Khan took Wazir with him to Lahore
and managed to get a full pardon.[31] Asaf Khan thereafter
became part of two important campaigns—the first against

the relentlessly rebellious Khan Zaman and the second in the bloody and brutal sacking of Chittor.

The pursuit and final destruction of Khan Zaman is interesting in this context for two reasons. First, because a stray comment made at this time suggests that Asaf Khan's sense of entitlement and his confidence that he would bounce back into the emperor's good graces probably had something to do with race. Bayazid mentions that when Asaf Khan was chosen as a commander of the imperial army sent to take down Khan Zaman, fellow general Khwaja Jahan bitingly commented that 'even a hair of Asaf Khan is more useful than the whole of the Chagtai clan'. Ouch!

But more importantly, the final battle with Khan Zaman gave Asaf Khan a chance to win back Akbar's trust. The *Maathir* says he showed enough 'loyalty and zeal' for Akbar to grant him the province of Biana as his fief in 1567 'in order that he might go there and make preparations and act as the advance force in the matter of Rana Udai Singh'.[32] Like Durgawati, Rana Udai Singh and later his son Rana Pratap refused to buckle under Akbar's bullying. It is curious that Asaf Khan was part of both the Battle of Narai Nala as well as the Siege of Chittor. Both battles bravely fought. Both blood-soaked. Both blots on Akbar's reputation as a tolerant and benign monarch. The massacre of around 30,000 common peasantry after the sack of Chittor is tinged with strong religious motivation, as the Fathnama-i-Chittor, a farman issued by Akbar in March 1568, proves. The farman quotes him saying, 'We spend our precious time to the best of our ability in war (ghaza) and jihad and with the help of eternal god, who is the supporter of our ever-increasing empire, we are busy in subjugating the localities, habitations, forts and towns which are under the possession of the infidels.'

In September 1567, the Mughal forces marched out against Mewar, and what followed was a four-month-long siege ending with a bloody carnage in which nearly 38,000 men were killed—8,000 warriors and the rest peasantry. The women of Chittor jumped into the jauhar fire, a repeat of what happened in Chauragarh just three years earlier.[33] The siege and sack of Chittor was one of the most brutal battles fought by Akbar. Abdul Majid, along with Wazir Khan, was in charge of the third battery charge against the fort and 'did excellent service' during the campaign, so much so that when the fort fell on 24 February 1568, 'the whole of sarkar of Chittor was assigned to Asaf Khan as his fief'.[34]

There is no definite mention of when Asaf Khan died. The man who stands bent-back before Akbar in the Miskin and Bhagwan painting from the *Akbarnama* sports a grey beard and looks well past his prime. He was certainly dead by the early 1570s because by the time the Gujarat campaign of 1573 began, we see a new noble holding the title of Asaf Khan—Khwaja Ghayasuddin. Historian and translator Henry Blochmann mentions on the margins of his personal copy of the *Ain-i-Akbari*[35] that 'according to an inscription on his tomb in Dihli, he died on September 14, 1569'. Khwaja Abdul Majid Asaf Khan was the perfect combination of pen, power and perfidy. The irony, though, is that the treasure he fought so hard to get his hands on, ruining a land and its people in the process, brought him nothing but fear and persecution.

10

Battle of Narai Nala, Part 1: Courage under Fire

'*Chandi roop dhari Maharani dono haath talwar/Bhagan lage Dilli ke sena Durga se payi na paar*'

(She is the very image of Goddess Chandi with swords in both hands/The soldiers from Delhi ran away, they couldn't face Queen Durga)

—Gond folk song

The ferocious face-off between Gond Rani Durgawati and Mughal general Asaf Khan in the Battle of Narai Nala was, in many ways, also a rivalry for reputation. While Asaf Khan came to the battle fresh from back-to-back victories in the region, the Veerangana rode into Narai Nala armed with the formidable track record of being unvanquished in battle. It is this reputation that Gond folk songs celebrate to this day with ballad after ballad eulogizing not only the queen's never-say-die courage in the battle of Narai Nala but also the bloody nose that she gave her imperial adversaries. As indomitable as her celestial counterpart, the queen is likened to the battle-fierce goddess Ran Chandi, whose valour crushes the invaders from Delhi. Indeed Rani Durgawati's great victory as a recurrent theme in Gond folk song is as entrenched today as it was more than four centuries ago. Take the catchy number '*Mor Durgawati O Garh Mandla Ki Rani*' by DJ Sarman, released in 2020. Its lyrics celebrate the queen's courage in protecting Gond honour and battle-pride: '*Dei Dei ho raj hamari Rani* (she gave us our rule),' goes the ditty adding, '*Gondon ki laaj bhachayi Rani* (she protected the honour of the Gonds)/ *Mughlon se tu lari larayi, Mughlon ko maar bhagayi Rani* (she fought with the Mughals and drove them away).' Clearly, what the song is referencing is a significant victory, so where and when did the queen achieve this? '*Lartay lartay Narai Nala pahuchi* (she fought on till she reached Narai Nala),' goes the song, ending with '*Pahuchay mari katari* (once there she cut down everyone).' Nor is that number an isolated example. In '*Ma Veerangana Durgawati Maharani*', a popular modern-day Gond ballad, bard Ramkumar Dhruva sings: '*Mughalo se woh ladi larai, kabhi haar na mani* (she fought hard against the Mughals and never conceded defeat).' Yet another song, '*Rani Durgawati Garh Mandla Ta Rani*' is more conventional, describing the queen as '*dukhiari*' or an unfortunate soul, but here too the focus is on her fight back or what the bard calls '*Mughal shashan say atul laraiyi* (heroic resistance to Mughal rule)'.

There's a reason why Gond bard song about the battle of Narai Nala is so emphatically celebratory. Like everything else connected to the queen, this too comes with history at its heart. To understand what happened in that narrow defile on a rain-swept June day nearly 460 years ago, we need to go back to how it all began. The Ramnagar inscription describes the battle of Narai as a tax collection drive: 'Asaf Khan, with an army, was deputed by King Akbar . . . for the purpose of levying a contribution,' it says.[1] While the soft-pedalling is understandable given the reduced muscle of the later Gond kings and the vassal–sovereign equation that they shared with the Mughal monarch of the day (the inscription likens Akbar to Partha/Arjuna and Asaf Khan to Bhima), there's a kernel of truth in that statement too. According to the *Akbarnama*, when the Mughal raids first started, they were little more than border skirmishes intended to scare the queen into submission. Asaf Khan 'began by attacking and plundering the villages and hamlets on the borders', says Abul Fazl.[2] Other historians also reiterate the nature of these strikes. Alexander Cunningham (in his *Report of a Tour in the Central Provinces and Lower Gangetic Doab in 1881–82*) calls Asaf Khan's attack a 'plundering expedition against Durgawati'. Khan knew he was taking on a kingdom that was helmed by a woman, but he clearly underestimated the queen's fortitude. The bullying did not work, and Durgawati refused to blink. The Gond Rani had endured enough border hit-and-runs during her reign to not react too much to Asaf Khan's antics.

Khan then decided an all-out attack would work better on the Gonds. His troops had just come off a couple of victories in the region and their morale was high. Armed with the young Shahenshah's orders, he collected what was by all accounts an impressive force—'10,000 cavalry and abundant infantry', not to mention a posse of top generals like Muhib Ali Khan, Muhammad Murad Khan, Wazir Khan, Babai

Qaqshai, Nazir Bahadur, Aq Muhammad, among 'a large number of holders of fiefs in that quarter' who accompanied him 'in accordance with the royal order', says Abul Fazl.[3] It was classic shock-and-awe tactic, intended to bludgeon the queen into submission.

Durgawati was expecting an attack but not quite the one that turned up at her doorstep with lightning speed. Abul Fazl blames the queen's arrogance and overconfidence for just how unprepared the Gond garrisons were: 'the Rani was drunken with the wine of negligence and was spending her time in prosperity,' he writes disparagingly. In reality, however, it was more a military miscalculation rather than negligence, as we shall see. When the Mughal contingent reached Damoh, 110 km from Jabalpur, Durgawati quickly assembled whatever troops she could to take on Asaf Khan. According to Abul Fazl, this is when the queen saw a large number of desertions. 'A stone of dispersal fell into the midst of her pride and her soldiers scattered in order to defend their families; not more than 500 men remained with her,' he writes.

That there was some confusion in the Raj Gond ranks at this point is undeniable. But that was more on account of the peculiarly federal structure of the Garha army. According to historian Suresh Mishra, the desertions that Durgawati faced during the Battle of Narai Nala were on account of the fact that her army was not well-organized and not all feudal lords were capable commanders who could boost the morale of the men. It is to their credit that the Gonds fought bravely even though they were not as well-equipped nor as well-trained as their Mughal adversaries. Local historians also say that while the swiftness with which the Mughal cavalry advanced took the Gonds by surprise, the real reason there were so few men at the queen's disposal to begin with was because of the decentralized nature of the Gond army. The rani would have faced difficulty assembling her troops, which were spread out among the far-flung fortress districts or garhs dotting her kingdom. As a land known for its rugged terrain and thick forests, Garha's first line of defence was always its topography, which is what Durgawati and her generals would have counted on to buy them some time. That the well-trained Mughal cavalry managed to neutralize that advantage would have taken the Gonds by surprise.

Despite her numerical disadvantage, the queen still wanted to give battle. Even Abul Fazl grudgingly admits that at no point did the rani's courage flag, even when the odds were impossibly stacked against her. 'As soon as she heard of the event the Rani in her courage proceeded towards the victorious army and with the rashness which outruns arrogance went forward to welcome a battle,' he writes. At this point, Durgawati's most trusted minister intervened and suggested an alternative strategy. Diwan Adhar Kayastha felt that the queen needed time to gather her forces and offer a more well-thought-out and better prepared resistance given the 'largeness' of the Mughal army.

The rani's initial reaction to that suggestion was angry disbelief. She felt that Adhar Kayastha, as the diwan of her kingdom, had not paid enough attention to the possibility of a sudden-death attack leaving the capital and the young king vulnerable. According to Abul Fazl, the rani remonstrated that the 'desertion was due to his stupidity'. Local historians agree that Kayastha may not have been totally blameless in this case—he clearly did not succeed in his diplomatic mission to the Mughal court, and his dependence on the Gond jagirdars and their decentralized troop management proved to be a major setback for Durgawati. Kayastha was excellent in civilian matters but he was no military mastermind.

Furious that she was being asked to flee from a fight, the queen demanded an explanation from her minister. She asked 'how she, who had for years governed the country, could resolve upon flight?' says Abul Fazl. Durgawati was clear about what she wanted to do: 'Twas better to die with glory than to live with ignominy.' The queen then asked Kayastha, 'What did that fellow [Asaf Khan] know of her rank? It was altogether best that she should die bravely.'

Abul Fazl's run-down about pride notwithstanding, Durgawati's reaction to Adhar Kayastha's suggestion does not smack of arrogance. If anything, it's pure courage under fire. The queen felt insulted that the Mughal dispensation was not according her the respect that's due to a sovereign monarch. Given that there was no hostility between Garha and the Mughal empire, she expected to be treated with the courtesy that a king shows a fellow royal even if he or she is a political rival. Her reaction, in fact, brings to mind the steely proclamation of another monarch from India's ancient past who demanded similar respect from his enemy—King Porus.

Despite pressure from her counsellors, the queen managed to collect a small force around her. By the time Asaf Khan halted at Damoh, the 'Rani had collected 2,000 men', says Abul Fazl, a four-fold increase from what she had to begin with, if we go by the *Akbarnama*'s estimates. But Adhar Kayastha was not the only senior member of her court who suggested Durgawati needed to live to fight another day. Given how cleverly the Gonds had used terrain to fight back attacks before, the counsellors wanted the Gond army to choose the where and the when of the battle. Abul Fazl gives a detailed account of how they convinced the rani: 'Her officers unanimously said that it was noble to determine upon war, but that it was not in accordance with courage and prudence to let fall the thread of deliberation. It was proper to stay in some secure place and to await the reassembling of their forces.'

The queen then decided to use her escape to mislead the enemy. She set forth for Damoh but stealthily changed course midway to completely disappear into the impenetrable forests surrounding Garha, leaving no trace behind for Asaf Khan's spies to pick up the scent. Meanwhile Khan, who had expected the queen to rush into battle and had been informed accordingly, was patiently waiting for the Gond army at Damoh only to realize he had been tricked. Abul Fazl as usual gives the details: 'Asaf Khan, who, on hearing that the Rani was approaching, had halted at Damoh, completely lost news of her, and though he sent out persons to make inquiries, yet, as the country was of an extraordinary nature, he could get no information.' The 'extraordinary' country that the *Akbarnama* refers to includes not just the rugged topography and thick forests which allowed the queen to disappear into thin air, but also the determined loyalty of her people, who protected her secret and made sure her trail remained cold long enough for her to regroup.

Durgawati and her men first made for the forests 'west of Gadha' and later the forests 'north of Gadha, and wandered about slowly in those deserts', says Abul Fazl. Obviously, Khan was livid that he had lost the queen and so decided to punish her by punishing her subjects. 'He advanced in person to Gadha and proceeded to bring the villages and hamlets into subjection,' records the *Akbarnama*. Durgawati, for her part, was waiting for more men to join her. She came to the end of her wanderings when she found the perfect spot where her much smaller army could take on the Mughal forces. 'At last she came to Narai which is east of Gadha,' writes Abul Fazl. 'It is a place very difficult for ingress or egress.' According to Sleeman, this spot was about 12 miles or 19 km from Jabalpur.

The *Akbarnama*'s description of this 'narrow defile' shows that the Gonds knew their terrain and chose their battle spot well. The ravine was surrounded by 'sky high mountains on four sides'. One end of the pass was skirted by the river Gaur, and at the other side was 'the furious river, the Narmada'. The access route to this valley was 'very narrow and awful,' says Abul Fazl. Like they did with Baz Bahadur, the Gonds wanted to trap the Mughal army into entering a pass secured by their snipers and elephant corps waiting to pick off the enemy soldiers entering in a single file. Besides, a narrow defile could, if defended well, keep out the big cannons that the Mughal forces came armed with. The Gonds had no cannons and little fire power, so they needed to neutralize the Mughal guns if they wanted a fighting chance.

By the time Asaf Khan finally got word of the rani's whereabouts, the queen and her army were already entrenched in Narai Nala. Khan did what the Gonds were hoping he would—he divided his army. 'When he got news of the Rani he left a force in Gadha and hastened after her,' writes Abul Fazl. Meanwhile, the weather started playing spoilsport. The rainy season had started and the pouring rain was turning the rugged passes slushy and impassable. Worse, both the Gaur and Narmada were swollen with flood water.

22 June 1564. Durgawati called her top officials to an emergency war council. News was out that the Mughal forces were on their way, and the rani wanted to give her commanders the option of opting out if they wanted to. As for herself, she would fight. Once again, the queen gave a rousing speech in favour of an all-out battle. 'She said that if they thought of going to some other place till her forces were collected, it would be proper to go but that her own inclination was to fight. Whoever liked to go might do so,' narrates the *Akbarnama*. 'Either she would fall or she would conquer.'

The queen's courage and determination convinced her generals and 'at last all men—there were about 5,000 collected—set their hearts on fighting,' writes Abul Fazl. Contemporary chroniclers say by the time of the final battle, the rani's resolve had managed to swell her forces considerably, even though there is still a fair bit of confusion about the final strength of the Gond army. Badauni puts the rani's troops at 20,000 horse and foot and 700 elephants, while Ferishta[4] says she fought with 1,500 elephants and 8,000 infantry and cavalry. There are similar differences about the Mughal strength as well: According to the *Tabaqat-i-Akbari* by Khwaja Nizamuddin Ahmad,[5] Asaf Khan attacked Durgawati with 5,000 horsemen and a large number of foot soldiers. However, Abul Fazl says 10,000 cavalry and other references (like V. Elliot in his translation of Badauni) put the number at 50,000. Keeping the numerical differences aside, it's clear that, even with reinforcements, Durgawati's army was still significantly smaller than the Mughal contingent. The silver lining, though, was that by this time the queen had managed to assemble some of her best generals by her side. Arjundas Bais, who was the faujdar in charge of the queen's famed elephant corps, was already positioned in the frontline. Fighting next to him were top generals like Senapati Chakraman, Kanur Kalyan Bakhila, Shams Khan Miyana, Mubarak Khan, Khan Jahan Dakit, Kharchali and Maharakh Brahman among others. The queen instructed Miyana Afghan general Bukhari Rumi and veteran commander Bhoj Kayesth to hold fort in the capital Chauragarh, and they fulfilled a very critical role after the battle as we shall see.

The Gond army was equipped with traditional weaponry. The *Prastab Ratnakar*[6] gives us a good idea of the kind of weapons they used—the *khadaga* broadsword, the *dhaal* or *charma* shield, the *gada* mace, the *mudgar* mace, bows and arrows, the *parushu* battle axe and the *kunta* spear, among others. The Gond army also used swords, daggers and matchlocks but, crucially, did not have cannons.

Since Narai is several miles from Singorgarh, its closest fortified bastion, the queen decided to position Arjundas Bais in charge of the first line of defence near Singorgarh. The rest of the force was arraigned near the ravine, waiting for the Mughal attack. Once the battle plans were laid out, there was nothing more to do but wait for news from the front. Folk traditions offer a picture of the royal enclosure in a battle camp. In *Folk Tales of Mahakoshal*, the story of

Lohabandha Raja describes the battle housing preferred by Gond royalty—'a tent with golden pegs' housed a 'golden mattress on the bed, the nails were of gold with pearl heads, the bedding was of silk'. Durgawati and Bir Narayan would have rested out that nail-biting night in enclosures not very different from this.

23 June 1564. Durgawati and Bir Narayan woke up early to prepare for what they thought would be a quick and decisive battle. Fond of meticulously following sacred rituals, the queen and her teenage son would have done what the *Prastab Ratnakar* prescribes[7] a monarch should on the day of the battle. They would bathe in the holy Narmada, wear white clothes and a *mangal tilak* (holy mark on the forehead) and pray to the Kula Devi Mata Chandi asking 'for her protection' and then 'worship the weapons with Raksha Mantra'. The morning puja done, they would slather their body with medicinal salves and then wear their armour. Breakfast would be light and, given the region's preference for millet, that would probably be on the menu as well as wild figs, *charchironji* berries, honey and ripe bel fruit, all part of a royal repast described in the *Folk Tales of Mahakoshal*.[8] After this, the mother-son duo would put on their *kavaj* (armlet) and, in a nod to the Mahabharata hero Karna, donate money and clothes to their generals and 'competent and deserving soldiers'. This done, they would 'take Vishnu's name' and wait for news from Singorgarh.

They didn't have to wait long, and the news was not good. Despite a spirited resistance, the Gond frontline had fallen, allowing the Mughal army to march towards Narai Nala. Abul Fazl describes it thus: 'News came that Nazir

Muhammad, Aq Muhammad and a large force of gallant
men had taken by force the head of the ravine which was
the road of access, and that Arjundas Bais had bravely lost
his life there.'[9] The setback would have doubtless upset the
queen, but she did not let it cloud her battle judgement. This
was the decisive moment to rally her men, and she did that
by leading the attack herself, astride her favourite elephant
Sarman, her glittering gilded howdah visible over the
infantry and cavalry crush on the ground. Gond folk songs
give a detailed description of just how majestic she looked
at that moment, the glint of her sword and the glitter of
her jewellery combining to create a vision of virulent beauty:
'*Hathon Ma sohay tarwar, bhala chamkat jaye*' sings the
bard, going on to add that she wore pearl necklaces, a gilded
belt and tied her long hair with beautiful trinkets, '*Garey
Ma pahiray munga motiya, kammar potiya sajaye/pawan Ma
sohay pejniya lambay kesh banaye.*' Thus bedecked, she gave
a rousing speech calling her men to war. The Gond soldiers
cheered lustily in return: '*Damak damak Rani garjay, fauji
de lalkar.*' This was textbook *rana-niti* or battle strategy—
when soldiers are all pumped up and full of *harsha*, says the
Prastab Ratnakar, it is a sure sign of victory (*jay lakshan*).
And so it was for the Gond garrisons. The bard describes
that adrenaline-pumping moment when eyes flashed fire
and the body was drenched in rivulets of blood: '*Akhiyan
se barsay agiya, tan se rakt ke dhar/Bairi dushman ke khatir,
fauji sabhi taiyar.*' The queen, says the song, looked like the
Goddess Kali herself, and her men fought fearlessly till the
hour of their victory brought a smile to the rani's lips: '*Jeet
ke danka bajaye ke, Mata manmuskaye.*'

Abul Fazl's description of what happened shows how effective Durgawati's tried-and-tested 'trap-and-ambush' strategy was. 'The Rani put armour on her breast and a helmet on her head and mounting an elephant slowly advanced to encounter the heroes who were eager for battle,' narrates the *Akbarnama*. Timing was everything. She needed the Mughal cavalry and infantry in the ravine before her elephants and snipers could pick them off and push them out. 'She said to her soldiers, "Do not hasten, let the enemy enter the pass and then we shall fall upon them from all sides and drive them off",' writes Abul Fazl.[10] Even in that narrow defile, the queen would have followed the half-moon, chariot or crocodile formations suggested by the *Prastab Ratnakar*, with the elephant corps in front, foot soldiers in the rear and the cavalry positioned along the flanks.[11]

The fighting was frenetic and bloody, but by close of day there was no doubt which side was winning. Even Abul Fazl admits that the Mughal attack was a disaster. Though the Gonds lost men too, Asaf Khan lost many more. Things, says the *Akbarnama*, indeed 'turned out as [Durgawati] anticipated, and there was a great fight. Many on both sides fell to the dust, and three hundred Mughals quaffed the wholesome draught of martyrdom'. In his epic poem about the rani, renowned local poet Acharya Bhagwat Dubey describes that scene of fierce and relentless savagery: '*Saikron dushman mare, samar bhoomi bahey shatru ke rudhir*' ('the enemy died in hundreds and the battleground was wet with spilled blood'). Unable to face the Gond charge, the Mughal army began to retreat with the rani at their heels. The queen, says the *Akbarnama*, 'pursued the fugitives, and emerged from the ravine' pushing the Mughal stragglers back to their camp. The verdict was clear: on day one of the battle, the 'Rani was victorious'.

This was a big win for the queen and, understandably, Gond morale would have been sky-high at this point. How important this victory was can be gauged from the way Gond bard song has remembered it. '*Naam Asaf dushman ke, gayish dhari dhari haar*', ('Asaf is the enemy and he loses the charge again and again') sings the Gond bard.[12] Contemporary Gondi singer and poet Manoj Maravi's hit song '*Mandla e Rani Durgawati*' also emphatically states that even Akbar's forces were unable to defeat Rani Durgawati: '*Jeet na payi Durgawati pe Akbar ke sena ghabraye*'. It adds that Asaf Khan's attack was by deception, and the queen drove his army out of Mandla: '*Dhokay say jab Asaf Khan nay Mandla mein kar di charayi/Aadhi sena badshahi ki Durga nahi gharayi/Durgawati mar mar ke sena mein bhagdar machayi.*' Even the Ramnagar inscription says that even though Asaf Khan was like 'a Bhima in prowess, whose armaments depressed the face of the earth', Durgawati 'vanquished his entire army'. Against all odds, the first day of the battle clearly belonged to Rani Durgawati and her Gond army. But as she returned to jubilation in her camp at sundown, the queen was too preoccupied to acknowledge all the cheering. She still had another day and another battle to get through. This meant she still had to neutralize the trump card in Asaf Khan's hand—the Mughal cannons.

11

The Battle of Narai Nala, Part 2: The Final Sacrifice

'Better to die with glory than to live with ignominy.'

—Rani Durgawati, *Akbarnama*

At the end of the first day of battle, the mood in the Mughal camp was, understandably enough, sombre. The defeat was a real snub to Mughal prestige. Worse, Asaf Khan knew his forces would face a similar fate the next day unless big cannons were pressed into service. Therefore, he instructed that the guns should be rolled into the valley during the night so that, by the time the fight began the next morning, they would be ready to fire.

Durgawati suspected this. The Gond rani knew that the day had gone her way, but she still needed to neutralize the Mughal guns. So, at sundown, the rani returned to her camp and called another war council meeting. The queen did not want to give Asaf Khan the time to move his cannons into the Narai valley. According to Abul Fazl, she 'summoned her chief men and asked what they advised', and 'each man spoke according to his understanding and courage'. The rani had a plan. She said, 'We ought to make an attack this night, and finish off the enemy,' records the *Akbarnama*. 'Otherwise Asaf Khan will come in the morning in person and take possession of the pass, and will fortify it with artillery. The task which is now easy will become difficult.' Unfortunately, night raids were neither easy nor common in medieval times, and the rani's commanders were reluctant to bet on so risky a venture. As they saw it, the Gonds had just won themselves a decisive victory. Why fritter it away on a gamble? So, 'no one agreed to this proposal', and faced with this reluctance, the rani 'yielded to the majority and retreated by the way she had come'," writes the Akbarnama. The queen then spent time with her men, honouring the dead and comforting the wounded. Then as now, Durgawati was a figure of veneration for the Gonds and, as she 'occupied herself in comforting those of her people who had been orphaned', the rank and file would have felt her inspiring presence.

When she returned to her personal quarters, the queen tried once more to convince the small group of generals who were most loyal to her. She was sure that even a small but committed force, armed with the crucial element of surprise, could foil any attempts by Asaf Khan to roll the cannons into the defile. 'When she came to her house she proposed the night-attack to some of her devoted followers,' writes Abul Fazl. But once again, 'not one of them could equal her in courage'. The queen had enough fire in her belly to try something out of the rulebook, but the men around her preferred caution instead.

24 June 1564. Morning dawned, bringing nothing but bad news for the Gonds. The sky looked dark and angry, the rivers were in spate and, on the ground, the Mughal guns were in position. 'When it was morning, what the Rani had foreseen occurred,' writes the *Akbarnama*. 'Asaf Khan came with his artillery and fortified the entrance to the pass', and the Mughal army 'entered the mountains'. Undaunted, the rani once again strode into the battlefield, exhorting her men to do their best. 'She drew up her forces, distributed the elephants and prepared for battle,' writes Abul Fazl. In her 'eagerness for battle', the queen 'mounted on a lofty and swift elephant which was the best of her animals, and was called Sarman, and came out'. The Ramnagar inscription offers a poetic description of what she looked like: 'Mounted on an elephant, in person and by force overmastering, in many a battle, prepotent adversaries, ever studious for safeguard of her subjects, she superseded to all appearance the protectors of the regions.'[1]

Once again, the battle was brutal and bloody. It started with arrow showers from both sides as well as gunfire, but soon got down and dirty with hand-to-hand combat. 'After the armies had encountered, the work passed from arrows and muskets to daggers and swords,' writes Abul Fazl, admitting that, once again, the Gonds acquitted themselves with honour. Bir Narayan, he writes, 'behaved bravely'. Other Gond generals such as Shams Khan Miyana and Mubarik Khan 'fought bravely'. It was a hard-fought battle, and it 'raged till the third watch of the day', which is late afternoon or early evening. Despite his guns, Asaf Khan could not dent the Gond defence thanks to the belligerent bravery of

Durgawati's teenage son, who was spearheading the frontline attack. The Mughal attack came in repeated waves, and each time the young king Bir Narayan pushed them back. Abul Fazl admits as much when he writes, 'The Rani's son . . . performed great deeds', going on to add that 'three times Raja Bir Sa repulsed the victorious army'. The third attack, though was vicious and, in trying to push it back, the young king was badly wounded. The queen saw that Bir Narayan needed to be quickly removed from the battlefield, so she 'ordered trusty men' to remove him 'to a place of safety; they obeyed the command and carried him off to a retired place'. The queen's instructions were clear: The king had to be taken to the safety of the impregnable Chauragarh Fort. He had to live to fight another day. Which he did, as we shall see.

For the Gond rank and file however, the sight of their king leaving the battlefield was a big blow. Till this point, morale was winning the day for the Gonds. Now, seeing their young king being carried away from the battlefield—certainly injured, gravely if not fatally—they lost their nerve. 'A great many left the field of battle and the Rani's troops were much discomfited,' writes the *Akbarnama*. 'Not more than 300 men remained with her.' But even then, Fazl admits, 'there was no weakening of the Rani's resolution and she continued to wage her war alongside of her own gallant followers'. By this time, a number of top Gond generals were already down. Among the commanders who were martyred during the Battle of Narai were Kanur Kalyan Bakhila (Bappola), Senapati Chakraman Kharchali, Shams Khan Miyana, Mubarak Khan, Khan Jahan Dakit and Maharakh Brahman. But the rani still fought on, exhorting her men to push the Mughals out of the ravine and save the day. The fighting continued till, in the dying hours of the battle, the queen ran out of luck. The rani, says the Ramnagar inscription, was already 'vexed with countless hostile arrows'. Those battle scratches didn't bother her too much till she took two back-to-back injuries.

This was a decisive moment in the battle of Narai—so decisive, in fact, that it has left its imprint on history. One of the most evocative illustrations in the *Akbarnama* is a painting by Keshav and Jagannath, currently displayed in the Victoria and Albert Museum, London. The picture captures the precise moment when Veerangana Durgawati began to take body blows during the battle of Narai Nala. Dated around thirty years after the fall of Durgawati, the painting shows the queen dressed in a printed *jama* and gilded chain-mail helmet, fighting from the glittering howdah of her elephant Sarman. A fierce battle is raging all around—her Gond archers are firing arrows from their long bows while her elephant corps is trying to cut through the sea of enemy soldiers blocking their way. The rani's troops are, at this point, hopelessly outnumbered and completely encircled by the Mughal cavalry and infantry, whose gleaming helmets and curved swords swarm the rest of the painting. It's a fearsome and frenetic scene, breathlessly brutal and almost photographic in its hurly burly details. Even as the fight clangs on around her, the rani is struck by an arrow. 'An arrow from the bow of fate struck her right temple, and she courageously drew it out and flung it from her,' writes Abul Fazl. But 'the point remained in the wound, and would not come out'. A seasoned warrior, the queen continued fighting disregarding the pain. 'Just then another arrow struck her neck,' writes Fazl. 'That, too, she drew out with the hand of courage, but the excessive pain made her swoon.' Bleeding profusely and faint from the injury, the queen slumped into her howdah seat.

As Durgawati fainted from loss of blood, her men fighting below would have watched in horror and wondered if she was already dead. An upright monarch clearly visible to the rank and file was the way medieval warfare ensured the fight continued and the men did not desert the battle midway. Those fighting on the ground had no way of figuring out whether their general was just injured or had in fact died. The queen knew this, and when she came to, she looked around her and realized the battle was already lost. Even her elephant Sarman was bleeding from the many battle wounds on his head and flanks as the picture from the *Akbarnama* shows. The rani's men, thinking her dead, were deserting in droves. Worse, the weather had turned nasty, and the Narai Nala was slowly getting flooded, cutting off her only chance of flight. Gond singer Manoj Maravi's song '*Mandla ke Rani Durgawati*' describes this moment: '*Pani barsay bijli chamkay aaye ge Nala mein baan*' ('It was raining in sheets and lightning rent the sky as the Narai started to flood'). Sleeman too talks about this: 'Rude tombs . . . cover all the ground . . . all the way back to the bed of the river, whose unseasonable rise prevented her retreat upon the garrison of Mundala.'[2]

With a sinking heart, the queen realized she was trapped. She could not retreat and she had no desire to be captured and humiliated by the enemy. Durgawati's motto, throughout the campaign, was death before dishonour.

Indeed, the *Akbarnama* quotes her saying, 'T'was better to die with glory than to live with ignominy.' As a woman, she was also anxious to protect herself from defilement by enemy soldiers. Gond folk songs mention this when they sing: '*Zakhmi chaut lagish tau Ma, Vahe raktan kay dhar/ Nari kay tan aaye vachahu, yehi haa ve mola saanch*' ('Even as you were bleeding to death O Mother, you wanted to protect the honour of your feminine form').

The queen was alone atop her elephant with only her trusted servant Adhar ('who was of the Bakhila caste' and therefore distinct from his namesake the prime minister) for company. When she recovered her senses, she addressed Adhar and asked him to do an impossible task. According to the *Akbarnama*, she said to him,

> I ever laboured to educate and consider you in order that one day you might be of service. To-day is a day in which I am overcome in battle. God forbid that I be also overcome in name and honour, and that I fall into the hands of the enemy; act like a faithful servant and dispose of me by this sharp dagger.

Adhar, like many of those closest to the rani, 'was distinguished for courage and devotion'. And his 'true heart could not do anything so hardhearted', writes Abul Fazl. He tried to dissuade his queen from this 'dreadful deed'. 'He said, "How can the hand which has held your gifts do such a dreadful deed?"' writes Abul Fazl. 'This I can do. I can carry you away from this fatal field. I have full confidence in this swift elephant.'

Durgawati was too battle-hardened not to realize this was a mixture of what the *Akbarnama* calls 'soft-heartedness' and optimism speaking. Adhar simply found the prospect of killing his beloved monarch too daunting a task, so he was promising her the impossible. By now, the Narai Nala was a death-trap, and any attempt on her part to try and leave the battlefield would invite blows on her elephant and a focused effort by Asaf Khan to capture her alive. And Durgawati had no intension of being captured alive. 'When the Rani heard these words, she grew angry and reproached him, saying, "Do you choose such a disgrace for me?"' writes the Akbarnama. But the horrified Adhar refused to raise a weapon on his own queen. For Durgawati, still bleeding and fast losing strength, time was running out. When the queen realized that nothing would make her faithful servant kill his monarch, she turned around and in a sudden movement 'snatched a dagger out of the girdle of the elephant driver and stabbed herself' in her abdomen, writes Ferishta. Abul Fazl's words capture this final moment of sacrifice when Gond Rani Veerangana Durgawati 'died in virile fashion', remaining till the very end a 'noble lady', the 'brilliancy' of whose 'rule was extinguished'. The *Akbarnama* painting brings out the soul of this moment of sacrifice, depicting Durgawati as a figure of desolate defiance surrounded by a vicious and relentless bloodletting.

Gond songs have repeatedly recreated the final battle of Narai, describing first the victorious Gond resistance and then the young king's injury and Durgawati's final charge and death. In many ways, the Battle of Narai was a moment in history that the people of Gondwana have held on to for nearly five centuries. Like the memory of the queen, the

memory of her final battle is now an intrinsic part of the
consciousness of the land she once called her own. So popular
is the legend of Veerangana Durgawati's battle bravery that
her story has been deftly woven into Gond epics and folklore,
where memory and magic have transformed history into
fantasy. In the legend of *Hirakhan Kshattri*, a Pradhan epic
from Gondwana, the brave raja who is 'lord of 8 and 20 forts
and sardar of 20' is pierced by arrows in battle mimicking the
queen's final moments. And like her, he 'fell senseless'. Of
course, Hirakhan then uses magic to revive and desolate the
enemy terrain of Bara Batti Bengala, cutting off 'the heads of
the Mussulmans'.[3] Similarly, in the folk tale of Raja Palibirwa,
Dalpati Shah is referenced thus: 'In Palipur Jhanjnagar there
lived Raja Singhisurwa, son of Parewa/Prem Shah, son of
Dalpat Shah.' In this story too, the queen is left behind a
young widow and faces a blood feud for the throne, not
unlike the power struggle Durgawati faced when Bir Narayan
was anointed king with her as regent.[4] Indeed, Alexander
Cunningham mentions Durgawati's myth magic, saying that
it is a 'characteristic' aspect of the queen 'whose memory is so
affectionately cherished by the people that everything related
to her is devoutly believed'.[5]

For the Mughals in general and Asaf Khan in particular,
Narai Nala 'was a great victory', not only because of the booty
it yielded but also because of how indomitable an opposition
Gond Rani Durgawati turned out to be. Among the war loot
that Khan laid his hands on was 1,000 elephants and 'much
other booty'. The Battle of Narai yielded a 'large amount of
property' and 'extensive territory' to the Mughal forces, but
Garha was yet to be fully conquered. Khan spent the next

two months subduing the Miyana country or what Abul Fazl calls 'Miyani wilayat', probably because of the number of Miyana Afghans who fought for Queen Durgawati. Besides, the monsoon was not the best time to attack a remote and rugged fort like Chauragarh, so Khan had no option but to wait it out. Historian Suresh Mishra also suggests that Asaf Khan took as long as he did to attack Chauragarh because some of the outlying Gond jagirdars may have mounted scattered guerilla attacks, which he needed to subdue. Either way, the two-month delay gave Bir Narayan time to recover from his injuries and recoup his forces. He knew that Asaf Khan would attack as soon as the rainy weather eased, so he prepared the defence of the fort accordingly.

By August, with his army rested and ready and the weather dry enough for battle, Asaf Khan set off to stake out Bir Narayan. What motivated him and his men was the promise of plunder. Chauragarh, says Abul Fazl, was 'replete with buried treasures and rare jewels'—the famed treasury of Garha, 'for the collection of which former rajahs had exerted themselves for many ages'. As gold lust combined with bloodlust, the Mughal army 'girded upon the loins of courage to capture this golden fort, and from the love of these treasures, they . . . eagerly followed Asaf Khan,' writes the *Akbarnama*.

Bir Narayan was expecting this, so when the enemy reached his doorstep, he decided on a do-or-die faceoff. The Gond army at his disposal was seriously depleted, and the young king knew this to be a suicide mission. So before leaving, he appointed Bhoj Kayesth and Mian Bukhari Rumi, the two veteran commanders in charge of the fort, to conduct a jauhar. 'These two faithful servants, who were the guardians of honour, executed this service,' writes Abul Fazl.

Bir Narayan's last act of courage did not save the fort or its inmates. The fort, says the *Akbarnama*, 'was taken after a short contest', and the young raja 'died bravely'. Two close members of Durgawati's family escaped the jauhar. 'Four days after they had set fire to that pile, and all that harvest of roses had been reduced to ashes, those who opened that door found two women alive,' writes Abul Fazl. 'A large piece of timber had screened them and protected them from the fire.' The two survivors were Kamlavati, the queen's sister, and the daughter of Raja Puragadha, who was the young king's betrothed. Both women, says the *Akbarnama* with undisguised satisfaction, were 'sent to kiss the threshold of the Shahenshah'.

Heartbreakingly, some contemporary references hint that Durgawati's dead body may have been desecrated by Asaf Khan and his men. In the *Muntakhab-ut-Tawarikh* (Vol. 2), Badauni says 'the happenings of her bad luck did not save her from ruffians'. This reference is followed by a veiled couplet: 'Every foul and fetid beast/Finds his foul fetid feast.'[6] The *Akbarnama*, however, is silent on this front. Local traditions continue to honour her memory by paying homage to her tomb which, says Sleeman, 'is still to be seen in a narrow defile between two hills'.[7] Gonds believe to this day that Sarman the elephant covered the queen's dead body with his own to protect her honour. Her son Bir Narayan was not so lucky—his memory hasn't survived the ravages of time, and his end was even more grisly than his mother's. According to Ferishta, when Asaf Khan took the fort by storm, Bir Narayan was 'trodden to death in the confusion'. The young king was not even twenty years old and was engaged to be married. History remains silent on the fate of his betrothed in the Mughal seraglio. The Battle of Narai signalled the end of Bir Narayan's nearly-decade-and-a-half glittering rule under Rani Durgawati's regency. The sun had set on Garha's glory days. For centuries afterwards, all that remained were memories—in songs, stories and stone. Nearly half a millennia later, that haunting hark back can still be heard when modern-day balladeer Manoj Marawi sings, *'Gondwana raj tun bachey ki haal?'* ('How will Gondwana survive without you?').

Garha under Rani Durgawati, was one of the two largest Hindu kingdoms in medieval India, the other being Vijayanagara. It is coincidental that their destruction also happened in quick succession: After the fall of Chauragarh in 1564, Vijayanagara was destroyed by the combined forces of the Deccani Sultanates in the battle of Talikota. The year was 1565.

Gone Glory: Garha after Durgawati

'In this kingdom of the English, how hard it is to live/In the village sits the landlord/In the gate sits the kotwar/In the garden sits the patwari/In the field sits the government/In this kingdom of the English, how hard it is to live.'[1]

—Gond folk song

Perhaps nothing captures the heartbreaking descent of Garha Mandla—from Durgawati's 'golden gourd' to a morass of disease and deprivation—better than the haunting folk songs from the Maikal Hills. Meticulously documented by Shamrao Hivale and Verrier Elwin in the early 1940s, these songs capture the miasma of despair that had by then enveloped the land of the Gonds. Rani Durgawati left behind an imprint not just on collective memory but also on the very fabric of her land. The political and economic stability that her rule ensured, in continuation of the reign of her father-in-law and husband, helped the later Raj Gond rulers carry on for the next hundred years or so, though with ever-shrinking military influence and resultant loss of terrain. From administrative structure, aspiration for Sanskrit scholarship to deft diplomacy, these later Gond rulers continued to reference the rani and take cues from her (and her father-in-law's) rule. This allowed them to survive the tumult of life under the Mughals, the Marathas and finally the British.

British rule came after centuries of invasion and instability, but perhaps this last cut was the bloodiest of all, because it casually disinherited the Gonds' claim to the forests that had always been their lifeline. Over time, famine and plague became part of the daily life of Gondwana. Indeed, the first recorded famine in the Mandla region in the nineteenth century, ominously and appropriately enough, happened in 1818, the year when the district was formally handed over to British administration following the third Anglo-Maratha War. Since then, grain scarcity and epidemics became increasingly common. By 1833, the price of grain, which was 400 seers per rupee just a few years ago, jumped to 8 seers per rupee in Raipur and 'in 1896–97, 1900, 1908 and 1921 there were serious disasters', write Hivale and Elwin in Folk Songs of the Maikal Hills.[2] Their account of what happened paints a disturbing picture of deprivation: 'Villagers have vivid memories of their sufferings in the early famines. Seed was hidden inside dung cakes for fear of theft. People would steal grain sown in the fields and eat it. They made *pej* [gruel] out of the dung of hares and bread of Semhar [silk cotton] flowers and wild figs.' Desperate and despondent, the Gond sang: 'Be careful where you go for the English are kings/Who has ever seen the boundary of their kingdom/They have taken all the best hills/ In the sweet forest they have built their bungalows/

They have big guns.'³ Along with hunger came disease. In their seminal book *Tribes and Castes of the Central Provinces of India*, R.V. Russel and Rai Bahadur Hiralal capture the hopelessness and misery that accompanied the plague outbreak in Mandla in 1911. Panic-stricken Gond villagers, fearing inoculation, threatened to axe-attack any government official who dared set foot on their land. A couple of years later, a cholera epidemic hit the region, and things got so bad that desperate Gonds abandoned the sick and dying in empty villages and sought refuge in the forests.

At the core of this desperation lay a colonial law that turned the centuries-old existing order of forage-and-tribute on its head. All through the Maratha rule, the zamindars who controlled the forest lands—under the Maratha sardars or chieftains like the Bhonslas, Holkars or Scindhias—did not restrict forest access. Instead, they bartered access in exchange for *bhet begar* (compulsory labour) and *bisaha* (compulsory foraging) as tribute. Bhet begar could involve carting loads or sowing and harvesting farmland for the zamindar, while bisaha meant sharing a part of forest forage as tax or even working for the zamindar to extract timber, honey and other produce. Because of the loose feudal structure in this region, the tribal populace often shared an almost familial relationship with their lords, who were seen as benign protectors. Gond folk songs repeatedly pit the blame for their suffering on the outsiders—the Mughals and the British— while celebrating acts of sacrifice and valour by local rulers such as Rani Durgawati and later Raja Shankar Shah and his son Raghunath Shah, who actively participated in the uprising of 1857 and were captured by the English, tied to the muzzle of a cannon and blown away. Interestingly, there are two Balidaan Diwas dates that Gonds celebrate to this day—the first, 24 June, commemorates Durgawati's sacrifice and the second, on 18 September, commemorates Shankar Shah and Raghunath Shah's martyrdom who also have a samadhi sthal of their own.

Although British efforts to land-map the region began almost immediately after 1818, the policies that caused this upheaval were implemented a little later. The support that local Gond rulers such as Shankar and Raghunath gave to the uprising must have contributed substantially to the way the British administration treated the region in the decades that followed 1857. In 1861, Gondwana became part of the Central Provinces under the chief commissionership of Sir Richard Temple of the Bengal Civil Service. Four years later, a forest department was set up to classify different types of forests and restrict access to 'reserved' areas. The British wanted exclusive control over forest produce like timber, but their classification of forests effectively cut the Gonds off large tracts of the best land where they were not allowed to forage, hunt or graze their cattle. With further curbs on traditional migratory agriculture and repeated laws that restricted the elbow room of local zamindars (many of them of tribal Gond or Baiga stock) on the lands they controlled, it's no wonder that the tribals thought of the *gora* or the white man as an exploiter.

Contemporary chroniclers accept that forest laws and other interventions kept the region deliberately impoverished. 'The primary occupation of the Gonds in former times was hunting and fishing but their opportunities in this respect have been greatly circumscribed by the conservation of the

game in government forests which was essential if it was not
to become extinct when the native shikaris had obtained fire
arms,' write Russel and Hiralal.[4] But if the ostensible reason
for keeping out Gond 'native shikaris' was conservation of
game, that same argument did not extend to British shikaris,
who not only continued to hunt but also bragged about how
easy it was to do so in this 'ultima thule of civilization'.[5]
A Central Province official called Henry Sharp, for instance,
casually mentions in his journal that the only silver lining in
what was a punishment posting in the middle of the jungle
was the unlimited hunting that Gondwana offered. 'There
are no limits, no marches—all the world is before you. You
wander where you will, and none can stop you; for there are
no game laws,'[6] he says.

Not surprisingly, local resentment first simmered and then
began to spill over. The first rumblings of discontent came
in 1887 from zamindars, whose powers were being gradually
chipped away by successive provincial announcements. In
1886, the chief commissioner introduced some new rules
for zamindaris under which they were placed directly under
the district commissioner. The zamindars had to sign an
agreement that they would comply by the rules both in the
administration of their lands as well as the forests under
their control. These rules gave the British more control over
zamindari forests and reduced the zamindars' ability to bypass
provincial diktats and rule their land independently. It also
allowed the British government to gobble up a large share of
the zamindari income. The zamindars of Gondwana did not
like this arrangement, and by 1890, many of them simply
refused to sign it. The provincial government responded

by conducting forest assessments, which caused widespread anger among all sections, as people started cribbing about 'government greed'. This bubbling discontent and the scattered protests it triggered later flared up into a full-fledged tribal movement in 1910, when the Marias of Bastar rebelled against the British administration. The Bastar uprising and its political impact quickly spread through the region, but it attracted a terrible reprisal in its wake—the colonial administration brutally suppressed it with mass floggings and public hangings. The rebellion and its aftermath completely eroded the influence of the local rulers, both over their British masters but, more crucially, over their own people.

Garha's deprivations may have reached a nadir during Company and later British rule, but things had actually started going downhill many centuries ago. The downfall of the region began with the death of Durgawati, the loot of Chauragarh and the vivisection of Garha Mandla. After capturing Chauragarh, Asaf Khan became governor of Garha. It didn't take him long to realize that the golden gourd was not easy to govern—it was a territory that was geographically diffuse, topographically inaccessible and politically restive. Therefore, Chandra Shah, the exiled younger brother of Dalpati Shah, was installed on the throne of Garha in exchange for 10 garhs or fortress districts: Raisen, Karubagh, Kurwai, Bhopal, Bhawraso, Garhgunnor, Bairagadh, Chowkigadh, Rahatgadh and Makrai.[7] Garha was now officially part of the empire as Garha Sarkar under Malwa suba.

Chandra Shah had an unremarkable rule, with real power being wielded by a succession of Mughal governors. Garha's spread and terrain needed the loose federal structure that Raj Gond monarchs followed. In contrast, Mughal administration was far more centralized. As discussed earlier, the attempt to integrate a tribal and remote region into the Mughal administrative structure was not particularly successful, and soon Garha turned into a revolving-door posting, with a succession of Mughal governors surviving short stints in the region. After twenty-five years of this, administrative and effective power reverted to the local rajas. For the next half-century, they governed the land with only intermittent interference from the empire as long as they paid their taxes and kept rebels quiet.

Both Sleeman and Cunningham maintain that Chandra Shah ruled for around twelve years. His end though, was bloody and unnatural. Poet Vittal Dixit says in the *Gadeshnripa Varnan Sangrah Shlokah* that the king and his older son and heir were murdered in Madan Mahal by his younger son Madhukar Shah, bringing the stain of patricide back to the family tree after more than half a century. So horrified was the court by this abominable act that Damodar Thakkur (brother of the celebrated Mahesh Thakkur) refused to anoint Madhukar Shah king. A peeved king retaliated by withdrawing the scholar's annual pension of 12,000 rupees, prompting Damodar to end his association with Garha and move to Darbhanga to live with his brother Mahesh Thakkur. Madhukar Shah ruled for over a decade and also became the first Raj Gond king to pay an official visit to the Mughal court. His death, according to the *Gadhesh*, was also unnatural—he immolated himself in a cave in Deogram near Mandla, though literary sources are silent on the reason why he chose to do so.

Madhukar Shah was succeeded by Prem Shah or Prem Narayan who, along with his son Hirday Shah, feature most commonly in Gond folk lore dating back to the years after Durgawati. Two separate titbits about them establish just how much Garha's relations with the Mughal court had changed since the Battle of Narai Nala. Like his father, Prem Shah also visited the Mughal court. Sometime in early November 1617, he gifted seven elephants to Jahangir, who in turn appointed him a mansabdar of 1,000 *zat* and 500 *sawar*. As for Hirday Shah, his brush with the imperial court was more romantic. As a musician of some renown, he was known to frequent the Mughal durbar, but when he fell in love with a courtesan there, he had to elope with her to Garha with some help from his diwan and raj purohit. This colourful story finds mention in a popular Gond folk tale, where the courtesan becomes a Mughal princess (in some stories she is Aurangzeb's daughter) called Chimni who married the Gond king, negotiated a peace deal between her father and her husband and finally came back to Garha to live with Hirday Shah. A contemporary literary work called *Chimni Charitam*, written by the seventeenth-century Sanskrit poet Nilkanth Shukla, has immortalized this love story.

Another popular Gond story shows Pemalshah (or Prem Shah) cleaning forests and ploughing the land with such ferocity that it caused the Mughal emperor's bed to slide. The emperor rushed to him and asked him to go to Garha Mandla because the land was fertile there and therefore easier to plough. In return, the Gond king had to pay a tribute of five pots of paddy and five pots of water chestnuts in a year. That modest rent, however, turns into a much steeper

tribute of 16,000 rupees demanded by Aurangzeb from
Hirday Shah when the two face off in the story over a pair
of golden slippers with the emperor's face imprinted on it.
The reference to elephants as imperial tribute from Garha in
Jahangir's memoirs *Tuzuk-i-Jahangiri* and the frequent details
of forest produce like honey, rice, water chestnuts and mahua
liquor as imperial tribute in Gond folk tales show that, by the
time Shah Jahan and later Aurangzeb became emperor, the
collections from Garha were mostly in kind and sometimes
not terribly substantial. That would also explain why Shah
Jahan and Aurangzeb used any opportunity they found to
extract ransom tributes from the region. Indeed, when Prem
Shah approached Shah Jahan for help against the Bundela
Raja Jujhar Singh of Orchha, who had attacked Chauragarh
in 1634, the emperor tried to use the plea as a ruse to raise
a hefty ransom. Initially, despite the Mughal emperor's
intervention, Singh continued the siege of Chauragarh, and
Prem Shah was killed while defending the fort. Hirday Shah
then once again approached Shah Jahan, who now imposed a
10,000-rupee fine on Jujhar Singh. It was when the Bundela
king ignored this diktat as well that Shah Jahan ordered
multiple campaigns against him, leading to the destruction of
the fort and ultimately the death of Jujhar Singh.

Chauragarh faced a number of attacks all through the
early decades of the seventeenth-century and was pretty
much in ruins by the mid-1600s, which is why Hirday Shah
had to set up a new capital city in the remote and forested
Ramnagar on the banks of the Narmada. Despite several
military upheavals—Hirday Shah also faced a later attack
ordered by Shah Jahan and was driven to take refuge with

the king of Rewa for a while—Prem Shah and Hirday Shah had long reigns covering nearly ninety years between them. Mughal interference in Garha's internal affairs, however, continued and intensified during Aurangzeb's rule.

Hirday Shah was followed by Chhatra Shah, who had a thirteen-year, mostly unremarkable rule. His successors were not quite so lucky though. Chhatra Shah was succeeded by his son Kesari Shah, who was ambushed and killed by his step uncle Hari Singh. Kesari Shah's infant son Narendra Shah fled and took refuge in Lanjhi. Hari Singh's perfidy did not go unpunished for long. Narendra Shah's supporters killed him in his sleep within three years. Hari Singh was succeeded by his son Pahar Singh who was finally defeated by Narendra Shah's followers. While this game of thrones and constant conspiracies kept things on the boil at home, the larger political picture also turned more turbulent when Aurangzeb kicked off his Deccan campaign in 1681. For nearly thirty years, there had been no imperial attacks on Garha, which was one reason why Hirday Shah and Chhatra Shah had reasonably long reigns. All that was now about to change.

Popular imagination has preserved bits and pieces of its memory of those turbulent times. Local legends say it was Aurangzeb's sword that vandalized the Kalachuri-era Chausath Yogini temple in Jabalpur, even though a bee attack stopped him from destroying the Gauri-Shankar murti in the inner sanctum. Similarly, there are local stories about Aurangzeb mutilating the murtis in Jabalpur's Pach Matha complex, another ancient temple connected in local memory with Rani Durgawati. So popular were these bee stories that Sleeman describes the legend in his *Rambles and Recollections of an Indian Official*: 'At Bherāgarh, the high priest of the temple told us that Aurangzēb and his soldiers knocked off the heads, arms and noses of all the idols, saying that "if they had really any of the godhead in them, they would assuredly now show it, and save themselves". But when they came to the door of Gaurī Sankar's apartments, they were attacked by a nest of hornets, that put the whole of the emperor's army to the rout.'[8] Gond legends also have numerous references to Aurangzeb, some innocuous and others downright unsavoury. But they preserve a few historical titbits, including Prem Shah and Hirday Shah's visit to the Mughal court and the constant pressure of higher tax tributes from Aurangzeb.

Typically, the Pemalshah or Prem Shah folk tales are fairly innocuous—either his virulent tilling of the soil prompts the emperor to come down to Garha and seek a tribute, or the Gond king is shown carrying mahua liquor and chiraunji nuts as gifts for Aurangzeb. In one story, Prem Shah so impresses the Mughal with his brain and brawn that he is given a princess in marriage. Of course, son-in-law or otherwise, once the Gond king becomes rich, the Mughal emperor comes asking for a 16,000-rupee ransom for his son Hirday Shah, who is taken to Delhi and placed in confinement. With Hirday Shah, the stories are nastier—he is confined in a well, he is spied on by a fakir sent by Aurangzeb, his city is attacked by Mughal forces and he is taken prisoner. Of course, the most common story about Hirday Shah is about his gold shoes with Aurangzeb's face imprinted on them. This footwear got the Gond king into trouble thanks to a gossipy official from the Mughal court called Bhagwatrai. Jealous of the prince, this sly official encouraged Hirday Shah to build a magnificent city with a beacon lamp. When news reached Aurangzeb—both of Gond prosperity as well as the gold shoes with his likeness imprinted on them—he wasn't amused and demanded 16 crore rupees as tribute. Hirday Shah refused to pay, defeated Mughal generals Ate Khan and Fateh Khan in battle, but was tricked and imprisoned when he went to the Mughal court on the emperor's invitation. The story of course ends with the Gond prince marrying Aurangzeb's daughter Chimni and living happily ever after. Folk tales apart, Aurangzeb's imprint on central India becomes evident from innumerable inscriptions that refer to his rule, from the Asirgarh Fort and gun jottings to the Amner tomb, Akola inscription and the sati inscriptions from Khimlasa.

Apart from the physical disruption caused by the Mughal army marching through this once-virgin terrain, Aurangzeb's Deccan campaign of just over a quarter of a century willy-nilly pulled Garha into the Mughal–Maratha crossfire. The seeds of Garha's later integration into the Maratha empire were sown at this time. And it was all thanks to Chhatrasal, the father of the beauteous Mastani. When Narendra Shah became king of Garha, defeating the usurper Pahar Singh, he sought imperial recognition of his claim and surrendered five forts (Dhamauni, Hata, Shahgarh, Garhakota, Madiyadau) in return.[9] The region was already on the boil due to the frequent clashes between Chhatrasal and the Mughal garrisons, and Garha's internal power struggle entered the fray when Pahar Singh joined the Mughal forces in an effort to win back the throne of Garha. And so, in an astonishing about turn, the Mughals turned around and backed Pahar Singh in his attack on Narendra Shah after first recognizing Shah's claim and tribute. Narendra Shah was defeated but very cleverly decided to bide his time. Once the imperial forces were too far south to offer Pahar Singh any support, he faced off the usurper again, this time killing him. That didn't stop Mughal interference though—the imperial commanders continued to needle the Gond king by offering support to Pahar Singh's sons, who conducted several uprisings against Narendra Shah. Indeed, Shah's entire forty-four-year reign was riddled with revolts, and he had to give up more territory to Chhatrasal when he sought his help to put out these conflagrations.

By then, the Marathas under Rajaram and Tarabai were fighting Aurangzeb all over the Deccan, and Garha's internal politics soon brought them into the picture as well. But the Maratha rule in Garha began in right earnest in the 1730s after the Battle of Bundelkhand. It was the swashbuckling Peshwa Baji Rao who first introduced Maratha power into Gondwana thanks to the entreaties of Bundela Raja Chhatrasal, father of Mastani. Chhatrasal had, for many years, locked horns with the Mughal subedar of Allahabad, Mohammad Khan Bangash. By December 1728, things came to a head, and Bangash attacked the Bundela Raja in Jaitpur, around 30 km west of Mahoba. An aged Chhatrasal realized he was horribly outnumbered and so sought help from the young Maratha commander at this point. Baji Rao very gallantly led a large army into Bundelkhand. After a pitched battle, the Maratha forces crushed the Mughal attack. A grateful Chhatrasal offered Baji Rao one-third of his kingdom as well as the hand of his daughter Mastani in marriage. Since Garha Mandla was practically next door, it soon became the centre of a tug of ambition between Baji Rao and Raghuji Bhonsla, who had been appointed by Chhatrapati Shahu to collect taxes in Berar and thus came to control the neighbouring Gond kingdom of Deogarh. Both Raghuji and Baji Rao wanted to annex Garha Mandla in order to extend their influence all over central India. By the time Raghuji went on his Allahabad campaign in 1739, he was already getting tributes from Maharajshah, who was then on the throne of Garha, though by then the kingdom was down to half of what it was under Rani Durgawati. Maharajshah controlled only 29 garhs as compared to the 52 garhs that comprised Garha under Sangram Shah and Durgawati.

After Baji Rao's death, his successor Balaji took on Raghuji and, armed with the Chhatrapati's authority to collect levies north of Narmada, attacked and annexed Garha in the summer of 1741. Maharajshah, says a letter written by Raghuji to Chhatrapati Shahu on 4 May 1742, committed *agni samadhi* and immolated himself on the funeral pyre to escape the disgrace of defeat. The incident, however, became a diplomatic hot potato, with a furious Raghuji complaining to Chhatrapati Shahu's representative in Satara that the peshwa was messing around where he did not belong. That kerfuffle stopped the peshwa from annexing Garha Mandla, though the next forty years of the kingdom saw its kings become more and more dependent on Maratha protection for survival.

The unfortunate Maharajshah was succeeded by Shivrajshah, who saw another Maratha attack and more loss of land during his short reign. Meanwhile, the neighbouring Gond kingdom of Deogarh had turned into a puppet state following several rounds of bloody internecine intrigue between the claimants to the throne. By the mid-1740s, Nagpur had become 'the centre of power in the region', says Suresh Mishra. The Bhonsla's writ ran over Chhindwara and Betul and large parts of Seoni, Balaghat and Hoshangabad, apart from Deogarh and Mandla. Shivrajshah's death saw more intrigue for the throne, and his step-brother Nizamshah finally took control of Garha after murdering the heir apparent Durjanshah in yet another blood-soaked power play. To be fair, though, Durjanshah's few-month-long rule was marked by chaos and brutality, so he did not have too many people backing his claim. Nizamshah's rule saw Garha become the centre of more conflict between the peshwa and the Bhonsla. This was particularly true since Janoji Raghuji, who succeeded Raghuji after his death in 1755, launched frequent raids into Garha Mandla, prompting the Gond king to send an emissary to Pune to negotiate peace and protection terms with the peshwa. Right through to the death of both Janoji and Peshwa Madhavrao in 1772, Garha Mandla's internal politics became entangled with the power play between the peshwa and the Bhonsla. The region had to pay the price for this political and economic instability. However, on the flip side, the constant rivalry between the peshwa and the Bhonsla allowed Nizamshah to deftly play both sides against the middle and keep his throne intact, as neither of the two Maratha powers allowed the other to completely annex the kingdom. Despite the dubious means he used to take over the throne, Nizamshah's rule was a relatively popular one. He is mentioned and remembered in Gond folklore and, like Dalapati and Durgawati, is known for refurbishing and expanding the region's waterworks and patronizing literature in his court.

Maratha control over the region spanned over eighty years, with local Gond rajas acting as their vassals or paying tributes to them. According to the *Imperial Gazetteer*, within forty years of the Battle of Bundelkhand, most of 'Garh had started paying tribute to the Nagpur Raja'. Between 1770 and 1803, the dominions of the Nagpur State included Garha Mandla, Gondwana and some of Rewa in the north, extending to Chhattisgarh and the dependencies of Surguja, Bastar and Orissa in the east and Berar in the west. The story of the last kings of the Raj Gond line is one of usurpation, intrigue and constant conspiracies for the throne, with rival factions using the power struggle between the peshwa and Bhonsla to destabilize both the dynasty and the kingdom. And yet, despite the intrigue and instability, things were not as desperate as they became once company and crown control came into the picture. As late as 1909, the *Central Provinces District Gazetteer* (Jabbulpore district, Vol. A) grudgingly admits about the region that the 'chief of Saugor' and 'the Raja of Berar' have 'not much impaired the prosperity which they found', adding that the 'thriving condition of the province, indicated by the appearance of its capital and confirmed by that of the districts' demands 'a tribute of praise to the ancient princes of the country'. That is fulsome praise indeed, though the *Gazetteer* later tempers that statement with some age-appropriate mumblings about 'Maratha misrule' and the 'exhausted and impoverished condition' of the people, painting the British as white knights come to the rescue.

After Nizam Shah's death, his widow Vilaskunwari backed his nephew Narharishah's claim for the throne. Nizam Shah's son Sumer Shah approached first the Bhonsla and then the peshwa for help to regain his legacy. Both sides demanded peace ransom from Narharishah, who refused to pay. As a result, with military help from the peshwa's man in Sagar Visaji Chandorkar, Sumer Shah finally ousted Narharishah after four years and became king. Sumer Shah's reign didn't last long however. When he incited local zamindars to a rebellion in an effort to free himself of Visaji's grip on his kingdom, he was defeated and imprisoned, and Narharishah was reinstated on the throne. The next seven years saw several skirmishes between the Marathas and the Raj Gonds, ending with Narharishah's imprisonment and death in 1789. After his death, the claim to the throne became a contentious one with both Narharishah's adopted son Narbadabaksh and Sumer Shah's son Shankar Shah offering themselves as the rightful heir.

Notwithstanding their own conflicting ambitions, however, both Narbadabaksh and Shankar Shah took up armed resistance against the British, the former in the 1842 Bundela uprising and the latter in the 1857 war of independence. To understand why both claimants to the Garha throne took on the firangi, we need to take a step back to understand ground realities in the decades between 1818 and 1857. As mentioned earlier in this chapter, British land laws were disastrous for Gondwana, and the entire heart of India was on the boil immediately after Company takeover. Dispossessed, disenchanted and desperate, local landlords of Gond, Lodhi and Bundela Rajput stock were simply at the end of their tether. The reason for this goes back to overtaxation. The British revenue settlement conducted after the third Anglo-Maratha War assessed land values at exorbitant rates. The tax amount thus fixed was simply impossible to pay. This caused the local jagirdars to repeatedly default, and a large number of them lost their land in the process. As a largely tribal belt, this entire region enjoyed significant economic and political autonomy under Maratha rule. Under Company rule, all of that freedom disappeared overnight, and people were reduced to unimaginable penury. Just how bad things were can be gauged from a contemporary account by an English civilian. Revenue officer Col. J.N.H. Maclean, who was conducting a reassessment in 1867 after Company control made way for the Crown, describes 'widespread misery and distress throughout', which 'must be seen to be appreciated'. The overall impression 'on inspecting these tracts was that the *pargunnahs* were dead, so vast was the desolation and so scarce the signs of life'.[10] Apart from ham-fisted tax greed, the region referred to as the Saugor and Narbudda territories saw several administrative flip-flops as well. It was first placed under an agent to the governor-general and then included in the North Western Province. After the Bundela Rising, it came back under a political agent. and it was finally included in the Central Provinces along with Nagpur state in 1861.

All of these factors contributed first to the Bundela rebellion and then to the much larger 1857 uprising. Although the Bundela Revolt was brutally put out, it continued to flare up for well over a year. And for the next fifteen years, as things got worse, the people got angrier. The local landlords stopped paying rents and encouraged their people to take up arms against the British. That groundswell finally culminated in 1857. Overtaxation led to repeated crop failures—famine, and disease devastated the region. The wheat crop failed in 1854, 1855 and 1856, says the *Madhya Pradesh Gazetteer*,[11] and this 'smouldering discontent then burst into the flames of 1857'. That Shankar Shah and his son would join the uprising is therefore entirely expected—by the mid-nineteenth century, life and property were in a precarious condition in Gondwana.

Despite being a colonial government mouthpiece, the *Central Provinces District Gazetteer*'s account of the impact of the martyrdom of Raja Shankar Shah and his son on the 52nd Native Infantry, the regiment in charge of the Jabalpur garrison, is quite telling. After they were 'blown away from guns, the adherents being reserved for the following day', it became clear that the sepoys of the 52nd regiment were deeply disturbed by this brutality. Despite some earnest moral whitewashing later that evening by their commandant officer Lieutenant Colonel Jamieson, who painted the Gond king and prince as 'criminals', the men were far from mollified, and the entire regiment walked out later that night, marching 20 miles or 32 km to join the rest of the company. Later, they 'respectfully' informed their colonel in Jabalpur that they were marching to Delhi to join the uprising.

Garha's fall from grace becomes quite glaring when one compares some of the revenue records from the Mughal, Maratha and British periods. According to the *Ain-i-Akbari*, under Mughal administration, Garha and the surrounding territory was divided into fifty-seven *mahals*, which yielded a combined revenue of 10,077,080 dams or over a crore copper coins annually. Compare this with what Abul Fazl says about Rani Durgawati—that her subjects paid their taxes and tributes either in gold coins or elephants and that Asaf Khan's loot from Chauragarh included 100 jars of gold coins and 1,000 elephants. As mentioned earlier, by this time Garha was no longer one of the top tax-paying territories under imperial command and performed much worse than smaller administrative units with fewer mahals.

By the time the Maratha period rolled in, revenue yield from entire central India (including Odisha and the Berar region of Maharashtra) was around one crore rupees. In his significant work *British Relations with the Nagpur State in the 18th Century*, C.U. Wills details that Garha Mandla along with Deogarh, Hoshangabad, Chauragarh, Multai, Gawilgarh, Narnala and Odisha constituted the territories 'directly under the Nagpur Raja', which 'yielded him a revenue of about 70 lakh rupees besides which he drew, probably, 30 lakhs as his share of the revenue of Berar'. This revenue count remained flat even under the British. In his first revenue report filed in 1861–62, just after taking over as the chief commissioner of the Central Provinces, Sir Richard Temple said that the total revenue from the Central Provinces was 80 lakh rupees. Between 1868–72, the annual income was 85 lakh rupees. Of course, revenue records over three centuries have to work in inflation and different coinage valuations, so these are not apple-to-apple comparisons. But even so, these three sets of data do make it quite clear that Garha's fortunes never really recovered after Durgawati's death on that rainy June day in 1564. The golden gourd was now just plain bitter. No wonder the Gond sang with self-snark,

'The Brahmin lives by his books,/The Panka boys run off with the Panka girls,/The Dhulia is happy with his basket/ The Ahir with his cows/But one bottle makes a Gond a governor/What matter if the Congress ignores us?'

Chapter 13

Remembering the Rani: The Queen Who Never Died

'Amar rahe Mata prithvi mein, ho jas rahe re tumhar/Rani Maharani jo aaye, Mata Durga jo aaye/Ran Ma jujho dhare tarwar, Mata Durga kahaye'

(May her name live forever on earth and her fame spread far and wide/Our Maharani, our Mother Durga/Valiant in battle with her sword unsheathed, she was called Mother Durga)[1]

Collective recall is a curious thing. It remembers some things, forgets others, and in the process, creates myths out of memories and legends out of lost stories. And so it is with Gond Rani Veerangana Durgawati. More than any other historical figure, she continues to live on in what was once Gondwana, her tale now part of the land she once ruled, her memory embedded in the popular consciousness. The people remember her with songs and stories—some true, some imagined and others halfway in between.

Veteran journalist Arvind Dubey is a familiar face on the streets of Jabalpur. Alongside stories about civic concerns and political developments, Dubey, currently bureau chief of the local Swaraj Express channel, routinely documents his city's heritage and the oral history that comes with it. That's what took him to the somewhat incongruously named Badshah Halwai Mandir (the moniker a reference to the charity of the sweetmeat-sellers that paid for the temple's upkeep and renovation) perched on top of a low hill in the Gwari Ghat suburb of Jabalpur. 'The assignment brought back memories of how we used to play in these caves when we were children,' remembers Dubey. 'I have grown up hearing stories of how there are hidden tunnels that connect this temple to the bathing ghat on the banks of the Narmada. Our elders told us those tunnels were built to ensure privacy for Rani Durgawati—so that she could take a dip in the river before offering prayers at the temple. No one ever found the tunnel and as children we would make plans to investigate but were ultimately spooked out.'

The tunnel stories are so deeply ingrained in popular imagination that almost everyone in Jabalpur has a version of it to offer. Raman Mehta, retired superintendent engineer of the MP State Electricity Board, has grown up in Jabalpur hearing these stories. 'When I was a little boy, we could see Madan Mahal from the terrace of our house, and most of the stories about it and the other forts associated with Rani Durgawati had to do with the underground network of tunnels that supposedly connected every fort and watchtower,' he says. And it was this clever connectivity, both for the queen and her soldiers, that kept invaders at bay for as long as it did, feel the locals.

School teacher Dr Shashi Saraf, who has spent a lifetime researching the rani, seconds that view. 'The popular belief is that there's a network of tunnels that once connected the major forts in the kingdom and a few of the queen's favourite temples so that Durgawati could travel in privacy from one fort to another and visit her favourite places of worship, like the Pach Matha Mandir in Adhartal, Chausath Yogini Temple in Bhedaghat or the Bajnamath tantric mandir in Garha,' says Saraf. 'People believe she seldom travelled over ground, preferring the quicker incognito route of her underground tunnels.' Local residents also firmly believe there was a network of tunnels that connected Singorgarh Fort with Madan Mahal, which was essentially a watch tower. This allowed the queen and her generals to plan a quick escape when faced with a siege and was one of the reasons why the fort was considered impregnable.

The tunnel stories represent some of the myths that the memory of Rani Durgawati has spawned. Stories like these resurrect the ghost of the Gond Veerangana through the mists of time. Every nook and cranny in the region bears a connection with her, and every ruined temple, fort or watch post comes with its own tale. Two centuries ago, Sleeman recorded the haunting story of the queen's battle drums frozen in stone and coming to life now and then, calling her long-dead soldiers back to battle. In the bits and pieces of history lying scattered all around Jabalpur and adjoining districts are lodged memories of another day; memories that the people, both Gond and otherwise, have held on to. Writing in 1916, clergyman-turned-chronicler Eyre Chatterton described this living memory succinctly in *The Story of Gondwana*: 'There are not wanting even today silent witnesses to the times when kings lived and ruled in Garha,' he wrote. 'Tanks built by many a Rajah, and especially by the famous Gond queen Durgavati; temples, now fast decaying, built to commemorate victories, or to propitiate gods and goddesses, vast plantations of mango trees planted by one famous Gond Rajah, all recall the bygone days of the greatness of Garha.'[2]

Much of this memory has metamorphosed into mythical stories, some spooky, others just plain fanciful. For instance, there are several ghoulish stories about Singorgarh Fort, though the really fantastic one concerns rumours of fabulous treasure, including a philosopher's stone, buried by Rani Durgawati in the hilltop tank. So popular are the stories of the *paras pathhar* or the philosopher's stone that some of the most well-known legends of Gondwana reference it. In the Pradhan Gondwana epic *Hirakhan Kshattri*,[3] the hero, who is called a 'true Raja of Gondwana', is shown to be in possession of this wondrous stone: 'There lived the true Raja of Gondwana/In the fort beneath a Pipal tree was the stone/ The Paras stone that turned iron to gold.'[4]

Paras stone aside, the tank in Singorgarh is the stuff of legend for another reason. Folk tradition has it that the rani's power has ensured that this tank never goes dry, and anyone who tries to dig for her treasure comes to grief. The stone and the tank represent two of the most abiding folk traditions about the rani. Most stories about Durgawati, apocryphal or otherwise, talk about either the prosperity of her reign or her munificence in making sure no one went thirsty in her realm. The popular tales about the waterworks that the queen constructed hark back to her reputation as an able administrator—a monarch who made sure her kingdom never faced a water shortage. 'In the mid-16th century, Jabalpur and surrounding areas had as many as 64 lakes and ponds,' says Saraf. Even after Durgawati, the tradition of preserving water bodies continued for the next 400 years. 'Even fifty years ago Jabalpur used to be a city of lakes, ponds and wells,' remembers academic Dr Subhash Chandra Sharma of Jabalpur's Rani Durgavati Vishwavidyalaya. 'Rani Durgawati is believed to have built many of these water bodies, including the famous Rani Tal named after her. The earlier water conservation system was excellent and the water tables were very high. Now rampant construction has robbed the city of both that heritage and the water security that came with it.' This destruction of water bodies becomes evident when you take a stroll through the city. Rani Tal, the lake built by the queen in her name, is now a mere pond. And yet, just over 100 years ago, Eyre Chatterton described it as 'one fine stretch of water between Jubbulpore and Garha' that 'still bears her name, the Rani Tal'.[5]

Other water bodies have fared no better. Adhar Tal, which was constructed by the queen for her trusted diwan Adhar Kayastha, is now Adhartal Talab. It's a ghost of its former self, and a nearby residential complex has eaten up a large part of it. Ditto for Cheri Tal, a tank constructed by Durgawati's *cheri* or lady in waiting, which has turned into a residential area, though it still bears its medieval heritage in its modern name. Says Dr Shashi Saraf, 'Earlier Garha was known as the land of "*bavan tal-bavan garhi*" [fifty-two lakes and fifty-two forts]. The queen was known for all the "*tal-talab*" [ponds and lakes] that she built, and this was one of the reasons why her people were devoted to her and revered her like a goddess.'

Of course there's a reason why the stories about magical water bodies continue to be popular in Jabalpur and surrounding areas to this day. For the rani as for her subjects, an important part of good governance was making sure the land and its people never went thirsty. The queen's focus on public works that made sure water was easily available makes sense given how often references to water, both for parched throats as well as for parched fields, crop up in Gond folk songs. Two examples illustrate this beautifully: 'In the front of the house is a Munga tree/Near the backdoor grows a bel/The river flows past the garden/So we will never die of thirst.' And then again: 'Where is the thunder? Where is the water that breaks through the clouds? O do not send me to the well for water . . .'[6] Trade and forest produce may have made Garha rich, but it was also a grain bowl and fruit basket as we have seen in earlier chapters. Irrigation and water management would therefore be a priority for any responsible ruler. For a monarch with a divine reputation, it would be top priority indeed.

Gond bard songs document this, giving it a semi-mythical colour and in the process turning the power-play between Akbar and Durgawati completely topsy turvy. In his Hindi biography *Rani Durgawati*, historian Dr Suresh Mishra talks about a folk song that describes the queen's magical powers over nature, which she uses to settle scores with Akbar. When confronted with lakhs of Mughal soldiers, horses and elephants, the rani simply invoked the river breeze, ordering it to spread fire and destruction in the Mughal camp ('*Pawan*

Ganga khey agya deho, deho jalaye'). Driven by the raging fire, Akbar is shown seeking refuge in the nearby forest, but here too the fire pursues him ('*Agey Akbar chare toriya, ohi ban lag gayi aag*'). At this point, a thirsty Akbar is shown looking to fill his golden pitcher with water, but wherever he goes, the water turns to stone ('*Jahan jahan Akbar bharey ghayalva, ohi patthar huye jaye*'). Suitably chastised, Akbar then seeks forgiveness from the rani, promising her that he would never molest her land again, and magically his pitcher fills up with water: '*Abki chuk bugs mori Mata, ab na awoo tere desh/Chatt ke bharey ghayalva Akbar, patt key laye uthaye.*'

Of course, Akbar never actually met the rani on the battlefield nor did her superpowers force him to seek forgiveness, but these songs establish the reverence that her people continue to have for Durgawati. According to Shamrao Hivale and Verrier Elwin, who meticulously documented Gond folk songs and poetry, these local references are important even when they take liberties with history because 'the songs are not all the evidence but they are an important part of it'.[7] The bits and pieces of history lodged in local memory are a pointer to what the locals thought worth remembering through the centuries.

A quick word here about how this focus on tal-talab was a tradition honoured by other Gond kingdoms as well. More than 160 years ago, Sir Richard Temple, the first British chief commissioner of what was then the newly minted Central Provinces, toured the region extensively. Eyre Chatterton describes his reaction to the water bodies dotting the area in *The Story of Gondwana*.

In 1865, after visiting the northern part of the Chanda district through which the Wainganga flows, and referring to a number of tanks which had been made by the old Gond Rajahs of Chanda in that district, Sir R Temple said, 'The number and size of these tanks is certainly remarkable. In some parts they cluster thick round the feet of the hills. From the summit of one hill, no less than thirty-seven tanks were visible. They are, as the people themselves told me, the very life of the place, and the object to which much of the industry and capital of the people are devoted. The two staple foods of the district, rice and sugar-cane, are entirely dependent on the water-supply from these tanks. Not only have these large sheets of water been formed by damming up streams with heavy earthwork dykes, but masonry escapes and sluices, and channels, have also been constructed. Some of the sluices, as headworks for irrigation channels, present an elaborate apparatus, creditable to the skill and ingenuity of the people.' [8]

For Gondwana, not just Garha, building tanks was as important as building temples.

Coming back to Durgawati, for the people of Jabalpur and the neighbouring districts, the queen's reign was a '*swarn yug*' says Dr Shashi Saraf. 'In popular imagination, it has become a time of plenty, when the land offered rich harvest, the forests teemed with wildlife and people paid their taxes in gold mohurs.' Durgawati's fifteen-year rule was the high noon of Gondwana, and much of the mythology around the queen is connected to the folk memories of those golden years. That is why, beyond ghostly sightings, buried treasure and dried-up lakes, Rani Durgawati's name crops up again and again as part of what can only be called living history.

Pankaj Patel, the young priest at the Sharada Mata Mandir near Madan Mahal, says he is the fifth generation from his family to be officiating at the temple. 'This temple was built by Rani Durgawati and the goddess was her Kuldevi or family deity,' he says. Legend has it that one night the goddess appeared in Durgawati's dream. '"I am roaming these hills; build me a temple here," she told Rani Durgawati and that's when the queen built this temple,' says Patel. Walk in today, and you will find, apart from a breathtaking view of Jabalpur city in the horizon, countless bright red flags festooned all over. This too is a living connect with the rani, who started the tradition of planting a wish-fulfilling pennant at the temple after her victory over Baz Bahadur.

That this tradition should endure for more than four centuries is entirely in the fitness of things. Part of the queen's appeal to this day is her reputation both as a protector as well as an efficient administrator. This combination of courage and concern is something that local bards celebrate and is part of the queen's quasi-divine reputation all over Gondwana. A Gond folk song actually describes how the rani could count upon celestial intervention in times of need, a reassuring quality in any sovereign.

Be our help on field of battle/For the Moghul army is coming/The daughter, the queen of the world says/Listen my little brother/Send for Indra's horse and arm it/And I will come with Sarada on my right hand/And Hanuman on my left/We will kill a hundred thousand Moghuls/ Two hundred thousand Moghul soldiers/Three hundred thousand Emperors/Be our help on the field of battle/For the Delhi Sultan has attacked us.[9]

Durgawati's fame as a monarch who offered both protection and prosperity lives on in other oral traditions as well, not all of them Gond. Take Acharya Bhagwat Dubey, a renowned and respected poet in the region. In his celebratory song about Durgawati, he highlights this twin appeal of the rani, suggesting that her popularity made Akbar jealous. The ability of these folk traditions to bend the historical power play between Durgawati and Akbar also becomes evident from the story documented by Alexander Cunningham, according to which 'the king of Delhi, when passing by Singorgarh, saw a lamp burning on the top of the fort'. He asked whose palace it was and, on being told that it belonged to a queen, sent her a golden cotton charkha as an appropriate present. In return, Durgawati sent him a '*pinjan* or cotton bow for cleaning cotton wool. This well-deserved retort so enraged the king that he marched at once with his whole army to fight the queen'.[10]

Modern-day Gond balladeers are clear why the memory of the rani is so important to the *samaj* (community). Manoj Marai, a Gond singer from a remote forest village in Dindori district of Madhya Pradesh, writes ballads about Raj Gond heroes, most notably Rani Durgawati and Raja Shankar Shah and Raghunath Shah. 'We celebrate Rani Durgawati's balidaan in June and Raja Shankar and Raghunath in September,' says Marawi. 'For the Gondi movement, these historical heroes are very important, and they are revered by the Gond samaj. Rani Durgawati fought against the Mughals, and Raja Shankar and Raghunath fought against the English. How can we Gonds forget their sacrifice?' For modern-day Gonds, the memory of their former glory is intrinsically connected to two major examples of heroic resistance: against the Mughals in 1564 and against the British in 1857.

Nor is this memory restricted to Madhya Pradesh alone. Durgawati's likeness crops up, most unexpectedly, far away from Jabalpur in the heart of what is now Chattisgarh. Heritage enthusiast Arjun Kumar, who has been photographing central India for decades now, was astounded when he came across a picture of Rani Durgawati displayed in the inner sanctum of a Shiv temple called Madwa Mahal (see picture). 'The temple is close to a larger shrine called the Bhoramdeo, about 133 km north west of Raipur,' says Kumar. 'The sanctum of the temple is in a depression, with its floor a couple of feet below the rest of the temple, and in a niche in this sanctum is a picture of Durgawati clearly cut out from a book or calendar.' The picture of the queen is displayed right next to a picture of her namesake, the Goddess Durga. Clearly, the tradition of deifying the rani isn't restricted only to the regions that were once part of her realm.

It is this divine reputation that has allowed Rani Durgawati, in popular imagination at least, to skip eras and take on adversaries a century apart. An example will illustrate this point. The Pach Matha complex in Jabalpur is a sixteenth-century temple that Rani Durgawati was known to visit. A curious organic structure, the temple structure is medieval with additions spanning centuries from late Maratha era to medieval to twenty-first century. The murtis worshipped here are just as varied—from Lakshmi to Shiv to Hanuman. But talk to the priest Mahant Akhilesh Puri Goswami, and he will tell you how many of the sculptures and murtis in the temple were mutilated by Aurangzeb en route to his Deccan campaign. 'What was left has been taken away to be displayed at museums,' he says.

This of course is not the only example of local memory remembering Aurangzeb. Jabalpur's famous Chausath Yogini temple bears the scars of his religious zeal, though there is a story about how the temple's central deity, Shankar and Parvati as a married couple, were left unharmed. Local legend says that Aurangzeb had declared he would destroy anything that did not make a sound to indicate it was a living being. He destroyed the yogini murtis, but was spooked away by the sound of a swarm of buzzing bees when he tried to desecrate the image of Shankar–Parvati. Alexander Cunningham has actually documented several of these Aurangzeb and bee attack stories, as mentioned in earlier chapters.

Both the Pach Matha and the Chausath Yogini temples are also intrinsically connected in local imagination to the memory of Rani Durgawati. There are countless stories of how she would visit these temples regularly, particularly on the eve of important battles or festivals. For the people of Jabalpur, the later desecration suffered by these temples has only reiterated the memory of the queen who stood up to Mughal bullying even if she battled an entirely different monarch in an entirely different era historically. Had Abul Fazl been alive, he would doubtless have been mortified at this time-lapse association between the man now celebrated as the most tolerant Mughal monarch and his least tolerant imperial descendant.

This tell-tale Mughal imprint on the local psyche is not just visible in temples alone. In *Folk Songs of the Maikal Hills*, Hivale and Elwin document a Gond love song with a Mughal-era memory embedded in it: 'My *jori*, my jori/The memory of your words/Impales my heart,' goes the song. 'The reference to the impalement of the heart is connected in the minds of these people with the punishments inflicted by the Moghals on their prisoners whom they sometimes impaled on stakes,' explain the writers.[11] Clearly, for the Gondwana locals, their memory of the Mughals has been shaped by the disruptive rule of a succession of imperial officials, none of whom enjoyed a long enough stint to care very much about the people under their control.

Worse, as the centuries wore on, like the ruined murtis in the temples and grisly images in their songs, the locals held on to the past more and more as their present became less and less worth celebrating. By the latter half of the nineteenth and early twentieth centuries, Gond oral traditions started documenting an even darker reality altogether. In contrast to the abundance of flora and fauna and references to copper and gold (coins) that crop up when the songs talked about the past, songs about their current reality often focused on famine, failed crops and crippling debt. A couple of these songs will illustrate just how dire their circumstances were: 'This is a year of famine/We are all dying of hunger/where shall we get our Kodon-Pej?/ Where shall we get Sikia-Pej? Take a leaf cup of Pej and be content with that.'[12] If you're wondering what kind of food pej is, here's a 1916 account telling you just how scanty this meal was. In their seminal work *Tribes and Castes of the Central Provinces of India*, R.V. Russel and Rai Bahadur Hiralal describe this meagre meal:

> The common food of the labouring Gond is a gruel of rice or small millet boiled in water, the quantity of water increasing in proportion to their poverty. This is about the cheapest kind of food on which a man can live and the quantity of grain taken in the form of this gruel or Pej is astonishingly small.[13]

And yet even this paltry pej was not always available, particularly when famine hit, as it did regularly in the last decades of the nineteenth and first decades of the twentieth century. Gond songs record the desperation of hunger in haunting words: 'Alas! Alas! This year how am I to feed my children?/For the crop has failed/I can pay my taxes by selling my plough and bullocks/But how am I to feed my children this year?'[14]

This persistent penury and the hopelessness that came with it meant that, for the Gonds, deliverance lay in remembering their glory days. The more miserable their present, the more they held on to the stories of gold and silver, valour and honour from their past. This was particularly true in the late nineteenth and early twentieth centuries, when British regulations deprived them of their traditional way of life, and famines became more and more common. The Gond remembered what was and how quickly that golden age dissolved into destitution and sang about it: 'The first Gond Rajas made forts of gold/They drank, they drank with their right hands/With their left hands they pulled down the forts/ Next morning they found their kingdoms were forgotten.'[15] This song, like many others, is a nod to the inexorable march of time, which can reduce the great and good to oblivion. Unless they live on in song and story, memory and myth. That's why, for the people of Gondwana, it is important to remember the rani. Because that is the only way the brave queen, who took her own life in a rain-washed battle many centuries ago, can live on, as she has for nearly 500 years. As long as her songs and stories reverberate through the length and breadth of her land, for her people, Veerangana Durgawati will always remain Gondwana's '*amar jyoti*'. Fierce feminine. Model monarch. Goddess.

14

Elegy of a Veerangana

The kingdom of the Gonds is gone,
But noble memories remain
And with a loving awe we can read,
The battle-page which ends the reign,
Durgavati.
When Asaf Khan with many men,
From Singorgarh through Garha drove
The stubborn Gonds, in a fast glen
Thou stood'st at bay and shook'st the glaive
Durgavati.
Their arrows filled the air with gleam,
Loud cannons made the gorge resound
And in the rear the treacherous stream
Swelled into flood and hope was drowned.
Durgavati.
Brave daughter of the Rajput blood
When the disaster noised thy pride

High as the howdah's golden hood,
Breasted a dagger's point and died
Durgavati.
The kingdom of the Gonds is gone,
And strangers rule o'er hill and plain
But never a stellar form has shone
The still lake which owns they reign
Durgavati.

By L.K. Lugard, first published in *The Pioneer* in 1871
(Excerpted from Ram Bharosh Agarwal's *Mandla Zilay Ke Adivasi Lokgeet*)

Notes

Chapter 1

1. W.H. Sleeman, *Rambles and Recollections of an Indian Official* (London: Humphrey Milford, 1915), 245.
2. W.H. Sleeman, *History of Gurha Mundala Rajas* (Bengal: Journal of the Asiatic Society, Vol. 6, 1837), 629.
3. Sleeman, *Rambles and Recollections*, 254.
4. Eyre Chatterton, *The Story of Gondwana* (Sir I. Pitman & sons Limited, 1916), 22.
5. Chatterton, *The Story of Gondwana*, 22.
6. Suresh Mishra, *Tribal Ascendancy in Central India: The Gond Kingdom of Garha* (Delhi: Manak Publications Pvt Ltd,2007), 224–25; Ram Bharosh Agarwal, *Garha Mandla ke Gond Raja*, 72–75.
7. Agarwal, *Garha Mandla ke Gond Raja*, 72–75.
8. Gond folk song from Suresh Mishra, *Rani Durgawati*, 71.
9. Mishra, *Tribal Ascendancy in Central India*, 220.
10. Abul Fazl, *Akbarnama,* trans. H. Beveridge (Calcutta: Royal Asiatic Society of Bengal, 1907), 334.

11. Abdul-Qadir Badauni, *Muntakhab-Ut-Tawarikh* Vol. 2, trans. W.H. Lowe (Calcutta: Royal Asiatic Society of Bengal, 1990), 65–66.
12. Khwaja Nizamuddin Ahmad, *Tabaqat-i-Akbari*, trans. B. De (Calcutta: Royal Asiatic Society of Bengal, 1939), 280–81.
13. Fazl, *Akbarnama* II, 323.
14. Mahomed Kasim Ferishta, *History of the Rise of the Mahomedan Power in India* Vol. 2, trans. John Briggs (Munshiram Manoharlal Publishers Pvt Ltd, 1981),217.
15. James Forsyth, *The Highlands of Central India* (London: Chapman & Hall, 1871), 83.
16. J.T. Blunt, *Early European Travellers in the Nagpur Territories* (Nagpur: Government Press, 1930), 215.
17. Forsyth, *The Highlands of Central India*, 16.
18. W.H. Sleeman, quoted in the *Central Provinces Gazetteer*, 225.
19. Chatterton, *The Story of Gondwana*, 21.

Chapter 2

1. James Forsyth quoting Gladwin's *Ayeen Akberee* II, 59.
2. Fazl, *Akbarnama* II, 323.
3. Ibid.
4. *The District Gazetteer of Jubbulpore*, 74.
5. Rodgers and Beveridge, *Memoirs of Jahangir* (London: Royal Asiatic Society, 1909), 379, 388.
6. Fazl, *Akbarnama* II, 332.
7. Fazl, *Akbarnama* II, 336.
8. Fazl, *Ain-i-Akbari* II, trans. Jarett (Calcutta: Asiatic Society of Bengal,1927), 210–11.

9. Shamrao Hivale and Verrier Elwin, *Songs of The Forest: Folk Poetry of the Gonds* (London: George Allen & Unwin Ltd, 1935), 57.

10. Mishra, *Tribal Ascendancy in Central India*, 239–41.

11. Fazl, *Ain-i-Akbari* I, 456.

12. Sleeman, *Rambles and Recollections of an Indian Official*, 245.

Chapter 3

1. Agarwal, *Garha Mandla ke Gond Raja*; P.N. Shrivastav, *Madhya Pradesh District Gazetteers: Damoh* (Bhopal: Department of District Gazetteers, 1974).

2. Sleeman, *History of Gurha Mundala Rajas*, 626–27.

3. Rupnath Jha and G.V. Bhave, *Nagpur University Journal* (1940), 181–201.

4. Sleeman, *History of the Gurha Mundala Rajas,* 625–626.

5. Fazl, *Akbarnama* II, 326.

6. Fazl, *Akbarnama* II, 325.

7. Fazl, *Akbarnama* II, 326.

8. Fazl, *Akbarnama* II, 326.

9. Hirananda Shastri, *Memoirs of the Archaeological Survey of India No.21 the Baghela Dynasty of Rewah* (Calcutta: Government of India, 1925), 6.

10. *Baburnama*, trans. Annette Susannah Beveridge (London: Luzac and Co., 1922), 562.

11. Shastri, *Memoirs of the Archaeological Survey of India No.21 the Baghela Dynasty of Rewah*, 3.

12. R.R. Bhargava, 'Coins of some Gond Rulers', *Numismatic Digest* 15, 119–21.

13. Mishra, *Tribal Ascendancy in Central India*, 265.

14. Fazl, *Akbarnama II*, 324.
15. Sleeman, *History of Gurha Mundala Rajas*, 627.
16. J. Allan, *Numismatic Chronicle & Journal of the Royal Numismatic Society* (1937), 310.

Chapter 4

1. Mahoba copper plate inscription, Dr Kalpana Jaiswal, Rani Durgavati Vishwavidyalaya.
2. R.V. Russel and Rai Bahadur Hiralal, *The Tribes and Castes of the Central Provinces of India* (London: Macmillan & Co. Ltd, 1916), 443.
3. Sleeman, *History of Gurha Mundala Rajas*, 627.
4. Ibid.
5. Mishra, *Tribal Ascendancy in Central India*, 308.
6. Sleeman, *History of Gurha Mundala Rajas*, 627.
7. Mishra, *Tribal Ascendancy in Central India*, 324.
8. G.V. Bhave, *Annals of the Bhandarkar Oriental Research Institute*, 28 (Poona: Bhandarkar Oriental Research Institute, July–October 1947), 254–55.
9. Ibid.
10. Fazl, *Akbarnama* II, 324.
11. Fazl, *Akbarnama* II, 326.
12. Stephen Fuchs, *The Gond and Bhumia of Eastern Mandla* (London: Asia Publishing House, 1960), 14.
13. Abbas Khan Sarwani, *Tarikh-i-Sher Shahi*, 723–24.

Chapter 5

1. Mishra, *Tribal Ascendancy in Central India*, 308.

2. Verrier Elwin, 'Kings and Battles', in *Folk Tales of Mahakoshal* (London: Oxford University Press, 1944).

3. Russel and Hiralal, *The Tribes and Castes of the Central Provinces of India*, 48.

4. *Madhya Pradesh District Gazetteers: Damoh*, 35.

5. Translated by Mishra.

6. Agarwal, *Gadha Mandla Ke Gond Raja*, 48.

7. Mishra, *Tribal Ascendancy in Central India*, 62.

8. Kalpana Jaiswal, *Rani Durgawati Aur Unka Shasankal* (Delhi: Northern Book Centre, 1998), 92.

9. *Bilaspur Gazetteer* (1910), 332.

10. Fazl, *Akbarnama* II, 327.

11. Ram Bharosh Agarwal, *Ranimata Durgawati*, 39.

12. Francis Buchanan, 506–07.

13. Pratap Kumar Mishra, *Mughal Samrat Akbar Aur Sanskrit I* (Varanasi: Akhil Bharatiya Muslim-Sanskrit Sanrakshan Evam Prachya Shodh Sansthan, 2012), 557.

14. *A Descriptive Catalogue of Manuscripts in Mithila I* (Patna: The Bihar and Orissa Research Society, 1927) 221; *Mithila Bhasha mai Itihas*, 16.

15. Fitz-Edward Hall, trans., 'On the Kings of Maṇḍala, As Commemorated in a Sanskrit Inscription Now First Printed in the Original Tongue' (*Journal of the American Oriental Society*, 1860), 14.

Chapter 6

1. Mishra, *Tribal Ascendancy in Central India*, 224.

2. Fazl, *Akbarnama* II, 324.

3. Mishra, *Tribal Ascendancy in Central India*, 62.

4. Balchandra Jain, *Proceedings of Indian History Congress—1959*, XXII, 262–63.

5. Fakirchand Akhara inscription.

6. Fazl, *Ain-i-Akbari* III, 451.

7. Fazl, *Ain-i-Akbari* III, 429.

8. Ishtiaq Ahmed Zilli, trans., *Proceedings of the Indian History Congress—1971*, XXXIII, 350–61.

9. Sharif–i-Usmani.

10. Alexander Cunningham, *Report of a Tour in the Central Provinces and Lower Gangetic Doab* 1881–82 (Delhi: Archaeological Survey of India), 101.

11. Ravishankar Shukla, *Abhinandan Granth*, 46.

12. Hall, trans., 'On the Kings of Maṇḍala, As Commemorated in a Sanskrit Inscription Now First Printed in the Original Tongue'.

13. Cunningham, *Report of a Tour in the Central Provinces* in 1873–74 & 1874–75, Vol. 9, 49–50.

14. Mishra, *Tribal Ascendancy in Central India*, 67.

15. Mishra, *Tribal Ascendancy in Central India*, 70.

Chapter 7

1. Fazl, *Akbarnama* II, 323.

2. Mishra, *Tribal Ascendancy in Central India*, 68.

3. Mishra, *Tribal Ascendancy in Central India*; Jaiswal, *Rani Durgawati Aur Unka Shasankal*; Shashi Saraf, PhD thesis.

4. Sleeman, *History of Gurha Mundala Rajas*, 45.

5. Shamrao Hivale and Verrier Elwin, *Folk Songs of the Maikal Hills* (London: Oxford University Press, 1944), 316.

6. Jaiswal, *Rani Durgawati Aur Unka Shasankal*, 121.
7. Mishra, *Tribal Ascendancy in Central India*, 309.
8. Cunningham, *Report of a Tour in the Central Provinces* in 1873–74 & 1874–75, 49–50.
9. Fazl, *Akbarnama* II, 331.
10. Mishra, *Tribal Ascendancy in Central India*, 194.
11. Hall, trans., 'On the Kings of Maṇḍala, As Commemorated in a Sanskrit Inscription Now First Printed in the Original Tongue'.
12. Padmanabha Misra Bhattacharya, 'Shloka 32', *Samayalok*.
13. Mishra, *Mughal Samrat Akbar Aur Sanskrit I*, 135.

Chapter 8

1. Agarwal, *Gadha Mandla ke Gond Raja*, 57.
2. Mishra, *Tribal Ascendancy in Central India*, 65–67.
3. Ferishta, *History of the Rise of the Mahomedan Power in India III*, 167.
4. Ferishta, *History of the Rise of the Mahomedan Power in India II*, 167.
5. Fazl, *Akbarnama* II, 327.
6. *Prastab Ratnakar*, 49.
7. Forsyth, *The Highlands of Central India*, 16.
8. Forsyth, *The Highlands of Central India*, 372.
9. Jaiswal, *Rani Durgawati Aur Unka Shashankal*, 114.
10. Hall, trans., 'On the Kings of Maṇḍala, As Commemorated in a Sanskrit Inscription Now First Printed in the Original Tongue', 14–15.

Chapter 9

1. Fazl, *Akbarnama* II, 182.
2. Fazl, *Akbarnama* II, 332.
3. Samsam-ud-daula, Shah Nawaz Khan, Abdul Hayy, *Maathir-ul-umara* I, H. Beveridge (trans.).
4. Ibid., 36.
5. Bayazid, *Tazkira-i-Humayun wa Akbar*, 176–87.
6. *Maathir-ul-Umara* I, 36.
7. Fazl, *Akbarnama* II, 168–69.
8. Fazl, *Akbarnama* II, 107.
9. W.H. Moreland, *The Agrarian System of Moslem India*, 239.
10. Fazl, *Ain-i-Akbari* III, 243.
11. Fazl, *Akbarnama* II, 231.
12. Fazl, *Akbarnama* II, 229.
13. Fazl, *Akbarnama* II, 230.
14. *Maathir-ul-Umara*, 37.
15. Ibid.
16. Cunningham, *Report of a Tour in the Central Provinces in 1873–74 & 1874–75, 49–50.*
17. Mishra, *Tribal Ascendancy in Central India*, 226.
18. Hall, trans., 'On the Kings of Maṇḍala, As Commemorated in a Sanskrit Inscription Now First Printed in the Original Tongue', 14.
19. Ferishta, *History of The Rise of The Mahomedan Power in India* II, 217–18.
20. Ahmad, *Tabaqat-i-Akbari*, 280.
21. *Maathir-ul-Umara*, 37.
22. Ahmad, *Tabaqat-i-Akbari*, 280–81.

23. *Maathir-ul-Umara*, 38.
24. Fazl, *Akbarnama* II, 332.
25. Fazl, *Ain-i-Akbari* II, H. Blochmann (trans.), 396–97.
26. Fazl, *Akbarnama* II, 382–83.
27. Fazl, *Akbarnama* II, 382.
28. Fazl, *Akbarnama* II, 404.
29. *Maathir-ul-Umara*, 38–39.
30. Fazl, *Ain-i-Akbari* II, H. Blochmann, trans., 396–97.
31. Fazl, *Ain-i-Akbari* II, H. Blochmann, trans., 396–97.
32. *Maathir-ul-Umara*, 39.
33. Fazl, *Akbarnama* II, 475.
34. *Maathir-ul-Umara*, 40.
35. Fazl, *Ain-i-Akbari* II, H. Blochmann (trans.), 368.

Chapter 10

1. Hall, trans., 'On the Kings of Maṇḍala, As Commemorated in a Sanskrit Inscription Now First Printed in the Original Tongue', 15.
2. Fazl, *Akbarnama* II, 327–28.
3. Fazl, *Akbarnama* II, 327–28.
4. Ferishta, *History of The Rise of The Mahomedan Power in India* II, 217–18.
5. Ahmad, *Tabaqat-i-Akbari*, 280–81.
6. *Prastab Ratnakar*, 75.
7. *Prastab Ratnakar*, 73, 75.
8. Elwin, 'History of Hirde Shah, a Pradhan story from Balaghat district', in *Folk Tales of Maha Koshal*.
9. Fazl, *Akbarnama* II, 327–28.
10. Fazl, *Akbarnama* II, 329.

11. *Prastab Ratnakar*, 81.

12. Mishra, *Tribal Ascendancy in Central India*, 226.

Chapter 11

1. Hall, trans., 'On the Kings of Maṇḍala, As Commemorated in a Sanskrit Inscription Now First Printed in the Original Tongue', 14–15.

2. *History of Gurha Mundala Rajas*

3. Hivale and Elwin, *Folk Songs of the Maikal Hills*, 390.

4. Elwin, 'Kings and Battles', in *Folk Tales of Maha Koshal*.

5. Cunningham, *Report of a Tour Through the Central Provinces in 1873–74 & 1874–75*, Volume 9, 54.

6. Mishra, *Tribal Ascendancy in Central India*, 81–82.

7. *Central Provinces Gazetteer*, 225.

Chapter 12

1. Hivale and Elwin, *Folk Songs of the Maikal Hills*, 316.

2. Hivale and Elwin, *Folk Songs of the Maikal Hills*, 309, 310.

3. Hivale and Elwin, *Folk Songs of the Maikal Hills*, 314.

4. Russell and Hiralal, *The Tribes and Castes of the Central Provinces of India,* 141; Hiralal, *Inscriptions in the Central Provinces and Berar* (Nagpur: Government Printing Press, 1932).

5. *Mandla Gazetteer* (1912).

6. Henry Sharp, *Good-Bye India* (London: Oxford University Press, 1946), 39.

7. *Gadhesh Nripa Varnan Sangraha Shlokah*, 264.

8. Sleeman, *Rambles and Recollections of an Indian Official*, 70.

9. Mishra, *Tribal Ascendancy in Central India*, 131.

10. *MP District Gazetteer Sagar—1967*, Vol. 35, 70–73.

11. Ibid.

Chapter 13

1. Gond folk song from Mishra, *Rani Durgawati*, 71.

2. Chatterton, *The Story of Gondwana*, 14.

3. Hivale and Elwin, *Folk Songs of the Maikal Hills*.

4. Hivale and Elwin, *Folk Songs of the Maikal Hills*, 362.

5. Chatterton, *The Story of Gondwana*, 23.

6. Hivale and Elwin, *Songs of the Forest: Folk Poetry of the Gonds*, 103, 87.

7. Hivale and Elwin, *Folk Songs of the Maikal Hills*.

8. Chatterton, *The Story of Gondwana*, 9–10.

9. Hivale and Elwin, *Folk Songs of the Maikal Hills*, 330.

10. Cunningham, *Report of a Tour in the Central Provinces in 1873–75,* Vol 9, 54.

11. Hivale and Elwin, *Folk Songs of the Maikal Hills*, 240.

12. Hivale and Elwin, *Folk Songs of the Maikal Hills*, 312.

13. Russell and Hiralal, *The Tribes and Castes of the Central Provinces of India*, 128.

14. Hivale and Elwin, *Songs of The Forest*, 56.

15. Hivale and Elwin, *Folk Songs of the Maikal Hills*, 317.

Bibliography

1. Agarwal, Ram Bharosh. *Gadha Mandla ke Gond Raja* (Hindi). Mandla, 1961.
2. Agarwal, Ram Bharosh. *Ranimata Durgawati* (Hindi). Mandla, 1997.
3. Aggarwal, Girija Shankar. *Gadhesha Nrpa Varnan Slokah Sangraha*. Mandla: Mandla Gondi Public Trust, 2003.
4. Ahmad, Khwaja Nizamuddin. *Tabaqat-i-Akbari*. Translated by Brajendranath De and Beni Prasad. Calcutta: Royal Asiatic Society of Bengal, 1927.
5. *Annals of the Bhandarkar Oriental Research Institute*, Vol. 28. Bhandarkar Oriental Research Institute, 1947.
6. Bayazid. *Tadhkira-i-Humayun*. Edited by Hidayat Husain.
7. Bhattacharya, Padmanabha Mishra. *Samayalok*. Kolkata: The Asiatic Society.
8. Bhave, G.V. *Gadhesh Nrpa Varnan Samagrah Slokah*. Nagpur, 1940. Translated by Suresh Mishra. New Delhi: Manak Publications, 2007.
9. Bhave, G.V. *Nagpur University Journal*. 1940.

10. *Bilaspur Gazetteer of 1910*

11. Blunt, J.T. *Narrative of a Journey from Mirzapur to Nagpur—Early European Travellers in the Nagpur Territories.* Nagpur: Nagpur Government Press, 1930.

12. Bose, N.S., *History of the Chandelas.*

13. Nelson, A.E., ed. *Central Provinces District Gazetteers— Raipur District.* Bombay: British India Press, 1909.

14. Chatterton, Eyre. *The Story of Gondwana.* London: Sir Issac Pitman & Sons, 1916.

15. Cunningham, Alexander. *Report of a Tour in the Central Provinces and Lower Gangetic Doab in 1881–82.* Calcutta: Office of the Superintendent of Government Printing, 1884.

16. Nelson, A.E., ed. *District Gazetteer Jubbulpore.* Bombay: Times Press,1909.

17. Eliot, Henry and John Dawson. *History of India as Told By Its Own Historians.* London: Trubner and Co., 1877.

18. Elwin, Verrier. *Folk Tales of Mahakoshal.* Oxford University Press, 1944.

19. Zilli, Ishtiaq Ahmed and Ishtiaq Ahmad Zill, trans. *Fathnama-i-Chitor, March 1568.* Indian History Congress, Vol. 33, 1971.

20. Fazl, Abul, *Ain-i-Akbari*, Vol. 2. Translated by H. Blockman & H.S. Jarrett. Calcutta: Royal Asiatic Society of Bengal, 1927.

21. Fazl, Abul, *Akbarnama* Vol. 1 & 2. Translated by H. Beveridge. Asiatic Society Calcutta, 1903 & 1907.

22. Fell, E. *Sanskrit Inscriptions; With Observations by H. H. Wilson, Asiatic Researches; or, Transactions of the Society Instituted in Bengal, for Enquiring into the History and*

Antiquities, the Arts, and Sciences, and Literature of Asia, Vol. XV. Serampore: The Mission Press, 1825.

23. Ferishta, Mohammad Kashim, *History of the Rise of Mahomedan Power in India*,Vol. 2.
Tarikh-i-Ferishta Vol. 2 Translated by John Briggs. Calcutta: R. Cambray & Co.,1909.

24. Forsyth, James. *The Highlands of Central India*. London: Chapman and Hall, 1871.

25. Guha, B.S. *Racial Elements in Indian Population*. Oxford University Press, 1944.

26. Habib, Irfan. *The Agrarian System of Mughal India—1556–1707*. 1963.

27. Hall, Fitz-Edward. 'On the Kings of Mandala, as Commemorated in a Sanskrit Inscription now First Printed in the Original Tongue', *Journal of the American Oriental Society*, Vol. 7.

28. Haridas, Karan Kulalankar Purushottam Putra, *Prastab Ratnakar*. Edited by Girija Shankar Aggarwal.

29. Hiralal, Rai Bahadur. *Inscriptions in Central Provinces and Berar*.

30. Hislop, Stephen. *Papers Relating to Aboriginal Tribes of the Central Provinces*.

31. Hivale, Shamrao and Verrier Elwin. *Folk Songs of the Maikal Hills*. London: Oxford Univeristy Press, 1944.

32. Hivale, Shamrao and Verrier Elwin. *Songs of the Forest: Folk Poetry of the Gonds*. London: George Allen & Unwin, 1935.

33. Hutton, J.H. *Census of India*. Delhi, 1933.

34. Jahangir. *Memoirs of Jahangir*. Translated by Rodgers and Beveridge.

Bibliography

35. Jain, Balchandra. *Proceedings of Indian History Congress—1959.*

36. Jaiswal, Kalpana, *Durgawati Aur Unka Shashankal* (Hindi). New Delhi: Northern Book Centre, 1998.

37. Khan, Shahnawaz. *Maathir-ul-Umara*. Translated by H. Beveridge. Kolkata: Asiatic Society, 1941.

38. Malcolm, John. *A Memoir of Central India including Malwa and Adjoining Provinces.* London: Kingsbury, Parbury & Allen, 1823.

39. Majumdar, D.N. *Races & Cultures of India.* Lucknow: Universal Publishers,1944.

40. McEldowney, Philip Fredric. *Colonial Administration and Social Developments in Middle India, The Central Provinces, 1861–1921.*

41. *Memoirs of the Archaeological Survey of India: 1925: The Baghela Dynasty of Rewa.*

42. Mishra, Pratap Kumar. *Mughal Samrat Akbar Aur Sanskrit*, Vol.1. Varanasi: Akhil Bharatiya Muslim–Sanskrit Sanrakshan Evam Prachya Shodh Sansthan, 2012.

43. Mishra, Suresh. *Rani Durgawati* (Hindi). Bhopal: Madhya Pradesh Hindi Granth Academy, 2012.

44. Mishra, Suresh. *Tribal Ascendancy in Central India: The Gond Kingdom of Garha.* New Delhi: Manak Publications, 2007.

45. Mukerji, Rai Bahadur A.C. *Heroines of Indian History.* Bombay, Calcutta, Madras: Oxford University Press, 1933.

46. Naik, T.B. *Gond Leadership—Adibasi 1965–66*, Vol. 7.

47. *Numismatic Chronicle & Journal of the Royal Numismatic Society* (1937).

48. Pathak, Ganesh Datta. *Garh Mandla Ka Puratan Itihas* (Hindi). Nagpur, 1905.

49. Russell, R.V. and Rai Bahadur Hiralal. *The Tribes & Castes of Central Provinces of India*. London: Macmillan and Co., 1916.

50. Sarkar, Jadunath. *The India of Aurangzeb*.

51. Sarwani, Abbas Khan. *Tarikh-i-Sher Shahi*.

52. Singh, Indrajit. *Gondwana and the Gonds*.

53. Singh, Jagat Bahadur. *Rani Durgawati Yugin Gondwana Ka Rajnitik Evam Sanskritik Itihas* (Hindi). PhD thesis: Ravishankar Vishwavidyalay, Raipur (MP), 1990.

54. Sleeman, W.H. 'History of Garha Mandla Rajahs'. *Journal of Asiatic Society of Bengal*. Calcutta, 1837.

55. Sleeman, W.H. *Rambles & Recollections of an Indian Official*. London: J. Hatchard & Son, 1844.

56. Smith, Vincent. *Akbar, The Great Mogul*. Oxford: Clarendon Press, 1917.

57. Srivastav, P.N. *Madhya Pradesh District Gazetteers—Damoh*. Jabalpur: District Gazetteers Department, 1974.

58. Thakkur, Mahesh. *Sarvadesh Vrityanta Sangraha* (Sanskrit). Edited by Pratap Kumar Mishra based on translations by Dr Subhadra Jha. Varanasi: Akhil Bharatiya Muslim–Sanskrit Sanrakshan Evam Prachya Shodh Sansthan, 2012.

59. Todd, James. *Annals & Antiquities of Rajasthan*. London, Edinburgh, Glasgow, New York, Toronto, Melbourne, Bombay: Humphrey Milford, Oxford University Press, 1920.

60. Varma, Vrindavan Lal. *Rani Durgawati* (Hindi). New Delhi: Prabhat Prakashan, 2020.

61. Ward, H.C.E. *Report on Revenue Settlement of Mundlah District 1868–69.* Bombay: Education Society Press, 1870.
62. Wills, C.U. *British Relations with the Nagpur State in the 18th century.* Nagpur: Nagpur Government Press, 1926.
63. Wills, C.U. *The Rajgond Maharajahs of Satpura Hills.* Nagpur: Nagpur Government Press, 1923.

Acknowledgements

Have you ever visited a place and felt a strange sense of serendipity—as if you've been there before, if not in this lifetime certainly in some other, a memory time-travel of sorts that blurs that line between experiences both lived in and legacy? For me, that place has always been Jabalpur. Even though I did not visit this city till I was well into my fifties, I have grown up feeling like I know it well. Part of the reason for that was how often my father mentioned his boyhood years here—the picnics, badminton games, trips to the Marble Rocks—and of course, endless descriptions of the gently flowing Narmada. When I first came across the story of Gond Rani Durgawati while researching another book, all those long-forgotten stories came rushing back and I suddenly felt as if I knew both the place and the person well. The Gond queen felt like a famous relative, someone you know through the stories you've heard about them. My first cursory research convinced me that this was a story I wanted to tell—as a modern woman I felt utterly inspired and not even a little intimidated by the queen's sheer spunk, her courage and compassion in an age more known for its rough-

231

and-tumble ruthlessness. She lived more than 450 years ago but Gond Rani Durgawati felt more twenty-first century than anyone I know.

When I began my research, once again serendipity kicked in. Every single cold call and mail elicited a reply and some help. The ever-helpful Professor Subhash Sharma, head of the department of history at the Rani Durgawati University in Jabalpur put me in touch with a number of local historians but his most important connection was Dr Suresh Mishra, the incredibly kind and generous historian who was an absolute authority on medieval history of central India. Dr Mishra took me under his wing—for no other reason except the fact that I was researching a place and people he held close to his heart. He helped me get my head around everything from field research, primary sources, manuscript hunts and digging for information in local legends and songs. He also helped me with the primary bibliography, put me in touch with local experts, worked on the transcripts of manuscripts that I came up with, exchanged notes with me on a daily basis and rooted for the book every step of the way. I have never seen a stalwart carry his erudition more lightly than this genial octogenarian historian. Unstinting in his help, unwavering in his encouragement, he became a father figure for me and when COVID–19 cruelly and suddenly claimed him in 2021, I felt bereft. This book would never have been possible without Dr Mishra's support and is dedicated to his memory.

As for Professor Subhash Sharma, his insight and interest in not just the history of Mandla and Jabalpur but the crumbling and fast disappearing heritage of the region is unparalleled and I am so grateful to him for his support for this book.

My thanks are also due to a number of Jabalpur historians including Professor Sudhakar Nath Mishra who helped me with contact details and Dr Shashi Saraf, whose knowledge of local legends surrounding the queen, perspective on tribal lives and livelihood, and knowledge of the social and economic status of medieval Gond kingdoms in central India, has helped me hone my narrative and structure my arguments better. I have quoted her and her research in the book.

When it came to field research, I relied on an intrepid young friend and researcher Aakanksha Bhatter, who helped me with the field interviews, sourcing of Gondi songs, reports on Balidaan Diwas celebrations, coordination with the ASI circle in Jabalpur and Mandla, sourcing of rare books from the Gondi Public Trust and even vox populi interviews of the local populace. I would like to thank her for the excellent inputs and all her help. She has since been accepted for an MA at a prestigious college in the US and I would like to wish her the very best going forward.

Thanks are also due to senior Jabalpur journalist Arvind Dubey whose video interviews and stories I have mined for local information and colour—a Jabalpur native, there aren't too many people in the city Mr Dubey doesn't know well and there aren't too many stories he hasn't already heard since boyhood. His perspective and inputs have been a critical part of my research. Mr Dubey also connected me with a fellow journalist—Virendra Sharma of India News Channel—whose amazing photographs contribute so much colour to this story of the Gond Queen.

I would also like to thank my dear friend and fellow heritage enthusiast Arjun Kumar, whose photographs have added historical depth to this narrative. Like me, he has been passionate about the history of central India and has been doing excellent work capturing crumbling heritage sites across Madhya Pradesh, Chhattisgarh, Bundelkhand and UP.

A thank you to Sheo Shekhar Shukla, IAS, principal secretary tourism, Madhya Pradesh, for allowing me to use photographs of Chauragarh and Singorgarh forts from the MP Tourism archive. These are critical to bringing the two forts connected with the queen alive on the pages of this book. But perhaps the most important picture—a seventeenth-century, near-contemporary portrait of Rani Durgawati—became available thanks to the support of S. A. Raman, IAS, director of Chennai Museum and his very helpful assistant, director R.D. Thulasi Brinda. Given that this is the only extant portrait of the queen (the battle scene in the *Akbarnama* shows Durgawati's last moments in a very busy tableau in which she is NOT center stage), this was a critical value addition and I am very grateful for this help.

I would also like to thank Dr Keka Banerjee of the Asiatic Society Kolkata who helped me source from the library's archives, an extremely rare sixteenth-century manuscript called *Samayalok*, commissioned by Queen Durgawati during her lifetime.

Thanks are also due to Vijay Aggarwal of the Gondi Public Trust, the archives team at the Bhandarkar Oriental Research Institute and my young friends and Sanskrit lovers in Pondicherry—Aneesh Raghavan and Aditya Maru who helped me transcribe some Sanskrit shlokas for reference.

Sourav Ghosh, a research scholar at the University of California at Berkeley has helped me with some of the bibliography references.

Sincere thanks also go out to my agent extraordinaire Kanishka Gupta of Writers Side whose faith in me has always been the wind beneath my wings and the wonderful team at Penguin India led by my editor Tarini Uppal whose expert eye and nose for nuance added both focus and depth to this narrative. May your tribe increase.

Last but not the least I would like to thank my brother Anindya Sengupta for painstakingly reading through the manuscript and offering suggestions as I went along, and my daughter Aura who routinely helped me with Sanskrit pronunciations and happily listened to me as I repeated the legends of Veerangana Durgawati over and over again—I would like think the Gond queen has left some imprint on her teenage mind.

To my readers, I say, go forth and rediscover your past. May serendipity guide you every step of the way just as it guided me—back to where the story began.